II

ELK COUNTY

MURDERS

&

Mysterious Deaths

Volume II

By James T. Baumgratz

IV

Copyright © 2019 by James T. Baumgratz

Printed in the United States of America

ISBN: 978-0-9708236-1-8

First Printing: February 2019
Second Printing: June 2019

Published by:

Baumgratz Publishing, LLC
P.O. Box 100
Ridgway, PA 15853

For my son Drew, the greatest accomplishment of my
life. Love you always.

CONTENTS

CONTENTS

FROM THE AUTHOR

Many of the cases you will read in this book are unsolved. The evidence was right in front of the investigators, but the technology to make use of it was many years from being invented. With the advent of DNA testing, many of the following cases could have been solved. If you are like me, you will find the arrest of Joseph DeAngelo as the Golden State Killer fascinating. I wait for the day the Zodiac killer is finally identified.

I write about local historical murders out of a thirst for history and the desire to know what our area was like in the not so distant past.

I am always aware that when I write about murders, I am writing about real people who suffered tremendously. Despite many requests, I tend to stay focused on murders that are from our distant past. I stay away from writing about cases that may have involved someone's father or brother or someone still alive. I prefer cases that happened many years ago, ones that are lost to the memory of time.

I hope you enjoy this second volume of true, local murders and mysterious deaths. This project, as I call it, took many hours and I am finally glad to complete this volume.

ELK COUNTY

MURDERS

&

Mysterious Deaths

Volume II

An Eye for an Eye

Cardiff around the time of the double homicide. The incident took place in front of these row houses.

This double murder takes us to the forgotten Village of Cardiff, located in Bennett's Valley near Force. It is one of the strangest and most raw examples of murder that ever took place in Elk County. I found the details of this case almost unbelievable in its progression and wonder how a simple, friendly wrestling match ended in a double homicide. As I write this sad story, I still cannot fathom how and why this case developed back in a beautiful spring day back in 1904.

Frank Paoli was described as a prominent merchant in the Hamlet of Cardiff around the turn of the century. He resided in the number sixteen company house, on the same street as practically all the other residents of that village. The first floor of his residence was a grocery store, where the local miners and residents could purchase staples, and his business was described as flourishing. As the village was very small, Paoli knew every resident on a first name basis, and every resident knew Frank. Frank, who was about forty-five years old in 1904, was married. His wife, Mrs. Paoli, was around forty-two years old. Together they had three children; the youngest was but an infant of fifteen months. The Paoli's had a stellar reputation in the village. The Saturday night of the incident started out as many others had. The residents of the company houses were all gathered in front of their homes, enjoying the warm weather and a break from the physical labor at the Shawmut Mining Company. Paoli went to visit the residents of company house number nine, where his good friends Saverio Pelligrino and Enrico Deponzian resided. Despite being from different areas of Italy, Paoli and Pelligrino had developed a close relationship and often engaged in friendly banter and shared stories and laughter at each meeting.

On this specific Saturday evening, the inmates of the boarding houses were holding wrestling matches in the front yards. In short order, a wrestling match was proposed between Paoli and Pelligrino. Paoli took off his hat and placed the hat along with his pipe on the ground, in preparation for the match. The match began as a normal affair, with both Pelligrino and Paoli exerting control, until Pelligrino overtook Paoli with an underhanded move and pinned him to the ground. Paoli loudly exclaimed that Pelligrino was a "cheater" and angry words were exchanged between the two. Paoli walked swiftly to his nearby residence, while Pelligrino retired to his second-floor bedroom at his house. When Paoli entered his residence, his wife noticed that he had a bloody nose and was missing his trademark hat. When she inquired about the missing hat, Paoli told her to forget about it, as he had left it in front of the Pelligrino boarding house. Mrs. Paoli volunteered to go and get his hat, and Paoli agreed, as he himself refused to walk back to the Pelligrino residence. Paoli stood on his front porch holding his fifteen-month-old child, while he observed his wife walk to the nearby residence. Mrs. Paoli stopped in front of the Pelligrino residence where her husband's hat lay.

As Mrs. Paoli began to reach down and secure the hat, Pelligrino yelled out of his second-floor window that he would shoot anyone who touched the hat. Mrs. Paoli ignored his threats and bent down. Before she could grab the hat, a shotgun discharged from Pelligrino's window, and Mrs. Paoli immediately collapsed, fatally wounded with a shotgun slug to the head. She died instantly. All of this took place right in the direct view of Frank Paoli. Paoli was incredulous at what he saw and immediately went into his store and placed his young child in her crib. He grabbed a pistol and shotgun and headed up to the Pelligrino residence, bound on revenge. Pelligrino, realizing what he had done, grabbed his personal items and headed down the stairs of his house, intent on escaping from Cardiff. He was met by Paoli bursting into the front door, armed with a pistol and a shotgun. Paoli, seeing Pelligrino on the steps, fired his pistol in his direction. The bullet missed Pelligrino and lodged in the wall. Paoli then began to swiftly climb the stairs, and he fired off another shot at Pelligrino, which also missed. Pelligrino headed back into his room and barricaded the door. Paoli attempted to break in the door but was unsuccessful due to the fact the Pelligrino had placed a heavy dresser in front of the door. Paoli gave up after a few minutes and decided to pretend he had left and hid in the shadows of the hallway, in hopes that Pelligrino would attempt to escape. Paoli made loud footsteps on the stairs as if he was leaving. He then quietly secured a spot in a dark corner, where he could aim his shotgun at the bedroom door. Paoli then waited for movement from Pelligrino.

In half an hour, Pelligrino had not heard a sound outside of his room. He decided to peak out, and if the coast was clear, he planned to make a run for it and hoped he could escape Cardiff and therefore escape justice. Pelligrino gingerly moved the dresser from in front of his door and quietly opened the door a crack. He stuck his head out the door and immediately was hit with a full shotgun blast to the head and was dead before his body hit the ground. Paoli had exacted his revenge. Paoli went to the body of Pelligrino and made sure he was dead. He then quietly went to the front of the house and picked up the deceased body of his wife and returned to his residence. The townsfolk, who had gathered around the body of his wife, followed him to his residence and surrounded his house in the belief that Paoli may attempt to escape. The authorities arrived in short order, and when they entered the Paoli residence, they found him cradling his dead wife and weeping uncontrollably. The constable, while sympathetic with Paoli, after hearing the sad story of the incident, also knew that he had to arrest Paoli. He told Paoli that he would have to accompany him to the Elk County Jail to await arraignment.

The body of Pelligrino was found lying in the doorway of his bedroom with its lower jaw nearly separated from his body. A coroner's inquest found that more than one hundred and fifty buck shots had taken effect in the dead man's head and neck. His face was mutilated beyond recognition. Dr. Hays was the one who conducted the autopsy. The dead man had a wife and two children in the old country and was employed by the Shawmut Mining Company. Pelligrino was about forty years of age when he met his demise. He was described as a troublesome character and the sentiment in Cardiff was totally against his memory.

The people of Cardiff, however, did not consider Paoli a cold-blooded killer and most even condoned his killing of Pelligrino, after the wanton killing of his wife. His neighbors and the village residents all combined resources to take care of the Paoli children, while Paoli languished in the jail. Many residents of Cardiff visited Paoli while he was an inmate in the jail and offered whatever assistance they could give. Paoli was described as a model inmate and awaited his fate in quiet mourning for his wife.

On Saturday, May 29th, 1904, Frank Paoli was taken in front of Elk County Judge Mayer for his writ of habeas corpus hearing. Judge Mayer declared that he would not have a man tried for such an act in his court and released Paoli from custody to be returned to his children. The case was officially closed.

Paoli returned to his children at Cardiff and eventually remarried and moved away. The body of his wife and Pelligrino were both buried in the Saint Joseph Cemetery in Force. The county authorities informed the Italian Consulate in Philadelphia of Pelligrino's death and they, in turn, informed his wife and children in Italy.

The question of why Pelligrino shot Mrs. Paoli over the hat will never have a logical explanation. I surmise that Pelligrino intended to fire a warning shot at the hat, but when Mrs. Paoli bent down at the same time he fired, she was hit by the slug. There is no other rational explanation as to what Pelligrino was thinking when he shot the shell that killed Mrs. Paoli. Although Pelligrino was described as of a troublesome character, no one who knew him thought of him as being capable of murder. The cold-hearted truth of the matter was that two people lost their lives that day over a common everyday hat. Life is indeed cheap and fragile and should be cherished with every waking moment.

The Demi-Mondes

Glen Hazel around the time of the "murders." The Bader house was located along the road leading to Saint Marys, which can be seen on the left of the picture.

Demi-monde refers to a group of people who live hedonistic lifestyles, usually in a flagrant and conspicuous manner. The term was commonly used in Europe from the nineteenth to the early twentieth century. In Glen Hazel, as in many other locales of Elk County, prostitutes and the men who visited them were often referred to as the demi-monde. A visit to one of these houses of ill repute, by two gentlemen, would prove deadly in 1899.

Mrs. Katie Bader and her daughter Kittie had come to Glen Hazel to set up operations sometime in the 1890s. Glen Hazel, at that time, was a booming town with many men employed in the timber industry, which was prevalent throughout Elk County. Men came from throughout America and Europe to gain employment in this industry and most came without family. They often toiled at physically demanding work up to eighty hours a week, and when the time came for them to enjoy a day off, they headed to the local taverns and "bawdy" houses. The men turned to these places to let off steam and find female companionship that they so desired, after spending all of their time with other men, in cramped lumber camp accommodations. The lumbermen were composed of all nationalities and were both black and white. Although African Americans were still considered second class citizens during this era, the need for men with strong physical capabilities trumped race, and they readily found employment. This is not to say that they did not find discrimination though, as their wages and living conditions were often lower and substandard as compared to their Caucasian co-workers.

A party was taking place on Saturday night, February 26th, 1899, in the Bader residence. Alcohol flowed freely, and the girls were willing. Initial reports were that the party continued into the early morning hours of Sunday when all went to sleep both intoxicated and exhausted. Katie awoke at around two in the morning and found her house filled with smoke. She quickly woke up her daughter Kittie and her two boarders, William Black and George Thompson, all of whom resided on the first floor. They hastily made their escape out the front door, as the stairway to the second floor was already filled with flames. Their escape was so sudden that they were unable to save anything from the structure, except the clothes on their backs. The group then went into the town of Glen Hazel to report the deadly fire.

They also reported that two men, Albert Reed, and George Taylor, did not escape from the fire. When local authorities reached the house, there was nothing left but smoking embers. Within the ashes could be seen the charred remains of both men. A message was sent to the Elk County Courthouse to call Coroner Mullhaupt, to come to the scene of the fire and hold an inquest over the charred remains. Coroner Mullhaupt impaneled a jury on Monday morning, February the 27th, and the findings of the jury were that both Reed and Taylor came to their deaths as a result of the fire and that the origin of the fire was unknown. Postmaster Wheeler of Wilcox was then given the charred remains, which he transported back to Wilcox. Wheeler had the remains buried in the potter's field above Wilcox. This would have ended the case, had rumors of foul play not surfaced before Mullhaupt had returned to his office.

In the following days, several witnesses came forward and stated they had heard one William Black, a colored man and a survivor of the inferno, make statements to the effect that the Bader house "would go up in flames." Black supposedly said these threats in the days immediately preceding the fire and his alleged reasoning was because he was in love with the young Kittie Bader and did not like sharing her affections with Albert Reed, a victim of the fire. Elk County District Attorney Wimmer now began an investigation into the fire and went to Glen Hazel to interview two alleged witnesses to these statements and to survey the remains of the Bader house. The Bader house was located roughly a mile from Glen Hazel on the Saint Marys Road. Today this area is heavily timbered. As the remains of both Reed and Taylor were already buried in Wilcox, he could not examine them for any signs of trauma. Coroner Mullhaupt told Wimmer that the remains were too disintegrated to find any evidence of murder.

The Bader ladies and their surviving tenants, both Black and Thompson, vehemently denied having anything to do with the fire and all denied arson was the cause of the fire. Wimmer, perhaps acting out of discrimination, filed arson and murder charges against William Black and had him arrested and transported to the Elk County Jail, to await trial at the April term of Court.

The trial of William Black began on Thursday, April 6th, 1899, in Ridgway with Judge Mayer presiding. The prosecution was presented by District Attorney Wimmer, and Attorney Shafer represented the defense. Wimmer began the prosecution by telling the jury that William Black was a known troublemaker, who had told two independent witnesses that the Bader house would go up in flames. Wimmer stated that the witnesses would testify to this statement. Wimmer also said he would prove that Black was in the residence when the fire began and that he, Black, was jealous of the affections Albert Reed, one of the victims, had been showing to the young Miss Kittie Bader, another resident of the house. Attorney Shafer stated for the defense that the two "witnesses" were known enemies of Black and their testimony was an outright lie and that all of the surviving victims of the fire would testify that Black never made such a statement. Shafer also said that even Coroner Mullhaupt could not say that the fire was arson. Judge Mayer then interrupted the trial to ask District Attorney Wimmer if he had any additional evidence that he would be presenting besides these two witnesses. When Wimmer replied in the negative, Mayer abruptly instructed the jury to bring in a verdict of not guilty against the defendant, William Black. Mayer also admonished Wimmer for bringing such a flimsy case to the Court and wasting the time of all involved. Wimmer was barely able to respond to the Judge before Mayer left the Courtroom.

Wimmer was, however, not willing to give up on this case. An anonymous resident of Saint Marys informed Wimmer that he should talk to a certain Norwegian, by the name of Fred Solveson, as he had information relating to the case and that the case was indeed a homicide. Immediately after the fire, the Bader ladies and their dispossessed tenants had moved into the residence of John Delige, which was located near Glen Hazel. Delige, a man of color, bore the same type of reputation as the Bader's, in that his house was also known as a house of ill repute. Solveson had gone to the Delige house on March the 27th, regarding some business dealings. Solveson stated that while he was visiting, Delige told him that the two men who had died in the fire were murdered. According to Delige, the white man Taylor and the man of color Reed had become involved in a fight about the girl, Kittie, in the upstairs bedroom and the white man had got the better of Reed. The matron, Mrs. Bader, shot and killed Taylor and then the house was set on fire and burned to the ground to destroy all evidence of the crime. Delige was picked up by the Elk County Sheriff's office on the charge of running a disorderly house, no doubt to try to get him to provide testimony for the prosecution relating to the "arson and murder" of the two gentlemen. Despite repeated attempts by Wimmer to get Delige to admit he made the statements to Solveson, Delige denied ever having told Solveson this story and said Solveson was known to drink to excess and often made up tales. Delige did plead guilty to the charge of running a house of ill repute and paid a small fine. Solveson, on the other hand, stood by his testimony and declared he would be willing to testify at any time and swear over a Bible that what Delige told him was the truth. Despite an exhaustive attempt by Wimmer to prepare a case against any of the survivors of the fire, he failed to put together a case that would be accepted by the Court. Concrete evidence was indeed lacking, and he only had hearsay testimony which could never prove beyond a reasonable doubt that this was arson and murder. No one was ever charged again over the deaths of Reed and Taylor, and this case remains a mystery to this day.

In researching this case, I could not understand how charges were ever brought against Black for something he allegedly stated. It was obvious that District Attorney Wimmer was grasping at straws to try to build a case against Black. Judge Mayer was correct in throwing out the case. Does a question also arise as to why the remains were left in the house for over twenty-four hours until the coroner arrived? Did the coroner ever check to see if there was a gunshot hole in either of the skeletons? As their remains were hastily buried in Wilcox, any secrets the corpses held were buried with them. The only information I found about Albert Reed was that he came to Glen Hazel from Olean, New York, shortly before the fire, and his family did not claim his remains. Taylor also had no known relatives in the area but was well known and liked by the residents of Glen Hazel. I also pondered the case of the Long girl and her lover, who burned to death on the other side of Glen Hazel around the same time as this fire, which I covered in the first volume. The Long girl had a reputation as a prostitute, and perhaps a vigilante was working in the area of Glen Hazel in 1899, who was targeting prostitutes. A similar house of ill repute was also torched in the following months on the way to Johnsonburg. Although this is circumstantial, I do believe all three arsons were related, and a serial arsonist was working in the area of Glen Hazel in 1899, and if they were ever identified, they were never prosecuted for these offenses.

Keg Killer

An old-time picture of "Centreville," in front of the Koch Hotel. Today this is in front of the Fox Senior Center on Main Street. This is where the assault began before the murder.

On October 4th, 1884, young Charles Peckham of Dagus Mines accompanied his mother into the town of Centreville (Kersey), to assist with her shopping for staples for their household. Charles was a boy of sixteen years old in 1884 and the pride of his mother. While Mrs. Peckham shopped, Charles hooked up with a group of five other boys aged between sixteen and twenty-one. The gangs of boys were later described as being of no good repute. As the young men caroused along Main Street in Centreville, they noticed residents drinking beer in front of the Koch Hotel. The group discussed how they would love to have a cold beer on such a warm autumn day. As they had no money between them, they decided to see if they could somehow swindle a beer or two from the establishment.

Frank Meyer was a recent immigrant to Centreville, coming from Germany. Frank had only arrived in America one year prior and had learned very little English. He was employed at the mines near Kersey and by all reports was a hard and determined worker. Meyer had come to America to follow his dream of owning a farm and someday bringing his betrothed from Germany to live with him in the states. Meyer had set out from his home near Earlyville on this October day to purchase a small keg of beer from the Koch Hotel. As he was walking to the Hotel, which was located along Main Street, he stopped and observed a festival that was taking place at the new school house, also located along Main Street. Meyer then proceeded to the Koch Hotel and purchased a small keg of beer. When he alighted from the porch of the Hotel and started back down Main Street, he found himself surrounded by a group of young men.

Peckham and his group were standing outside of the Koch Hotel when they observed the young Frank Meyer enter the establishment. When Meyer exited the Hotel carrying a keg of beer the boys all looked at each other and decided to rob Meyer of his beer and thereby satisfy their thirst. They immediately surrounded Meyer and attempted to take the keg from his shoulders. Meyer, realizing what they were trying to do, yelled out in alarm, loud enough for some of the participants at the festival to hear and these people began to look in his direction. The gang decided to wait until Meyer went further down the street to attack again. Meyer meanwhile swiftly took off down Main Street with the gang in hot pursuit. When Meyer came to the George Hoose establishment, he entered the porch and began to pound on the door asking for help. When no one came to his rescue, he put the keg down and sat on it, warning the now encircled gang that he would not give up the beer and at the same time he brandished a large knife from his pocket. One member of the gang came in close to try to knock him off the keg and received a cut to his hand. Peckham then came at Meyer, and in an instant, Meyer swung his knife and Peckham received a deep cut to the throat. Blood immediately began to flow from the young Peckham's throat, and his gang now rushed him to the nearby porch of Esquire Luther, but Peckham died on the Luther porch before medical help could be summoned. Esquire Luther summoned the Elk County Authorities, and the Sheriff arrived and arrested Meyer and transported him to the jail. Luther then formed a coroner's jury consisting of John Collins, Patrick Callihan, Walter Meredith, John Baily, George Boyer, and Frank Straessley. Elk County Coroner Dr. E. T. Williams and Dr. S. M. Free then proceeded to make a post mortem examination and found that the windpipe had received about half the blow and at the same time the cut severed one of the adjoining arteries. Death was within ten minutes. The jury rendered its verdict that Charles Peckham had died as a result of a homicide committed by one Francis Meyer. The body of the young Peckham had lain on the porch of Luther's office the whole time this inquest was held and only late in the afternoon was the body sent home to a grieving mother.

Meyer languished in the Elk County Jail until the January term of Court which was held on the 26th in 1885. Meyer was given a translator due to his limited understanding of the English language and expressed remorse for the young Peckham's death. He decided to plead guilty to the charge of voluntary manslaughter and accepted the Court's sentence of one year and three months hard labor at the Western Penitentiary. Meyer returned to the area after his imprisonment and went on to become quite a successful farmer. Peckham was buried in the family plot at the Elkton Cemetery, not far from where he received his fatal wound.

A few notes on this case. The late Carol Dornisch of Saint Marys told me about this murder many years ago. She said every father's day when she visited her father's grave with her mother; she would also place a flower on young Charlie Peckham's grave. She was told he by her mother that Charlie was an innocent victim of a murder. When I researched the case, I told her Charlie was not an innocent victim, and she was surprised that all the years she went to his grave; she never knew the whole story. I would think that in today's Court system, Meyer would not have been charged with voluntary manslaughter as he was defending his property. He did express remorse for what happened, but in reality, he is not the one who caused the incident in the first place. The names of the other disreputable youths that participated in this incident were not recorded, but none of them were charged with any crimes. They should probably have been charged as accessories to this murder, as they were just as involved as Peckham in the attempt to steal the beer.

Little Charlie Peckham's grave located next to the
Kersey Community building in the Elkton Cemetery.

Politics

The Horton Township sign located on the Boot Jack Summit. The Phalen's farm was located on the left, back in 1874.

On July 19th, 1874, the Democratic Party of Elk County was holding their annual primary meeting at the Oyster Hotel in Horton Township. One of the main topics at the meeting was the choosing of the Democratic Parties' candidate for Elk County Treasurer. The position was contested between one Windfelder (incumbent) and one G. G. Messenger. The meeting was held in the banquet room of the hotel, with many participants imbibing in alcohol throughout the long Saturday afternoon and evening. The meeting broke up around eight o'clock at night, and the parties began venturing towards their respective dwellings. There were reportedly loud arguments throughout the day and some of these continued on the way home.

One such party, which consisted of William Phalen, his son James Phalen, William Bromley and his son John and Dennis Donovan and his son James, all had spent the day drinking and arguing about the position of the candidate for the Elk County Treasurer. William Bromley accused James Phalen of receiving money from Windfelder (a candidate) and in turn working for his campaign. Phalen, in turn, accused William Bromley of receiving money from Messenger (the other candidate) for the same purpose. Both Bromley and Phalen were the elected delegates for their areas, and if they received "slush" money to support one or the other candidate, it would be scandalous. This fight had carried on throughout the day.

The group had set out on horses and wagons from the Oyster Hotel headed towards Ridgway. The Donovans were on horseback, and the Phalens and Bromleys were in wagons. William Phalen attempted to pass the Bromley wagon. Bromley turned his wagon sideways to prevent the Phalen wagon from passing him. This continued back and forth until the party reached the Phalen house, which was located on present-day Boot Jack Hill. William Phalen attempted to turn into his driveway, and Bromley attempted to block his access once again. The aged Phalen finally was able to drive his wagon into his yard, outwitting Bromley's roadblock. Bromley then alighted from his wagon and handed the reins to his son John and proceeded to follow the old Phalen into his yard on foot. Bromley continued his loud verbal abuse of Phalen in the latter's yard. Bromley was told to leave the Phalen's property and to leave the old man alone. Bromley refused to leave the property and continued his verbal assault.

James Phalen then threatened Bromley that if he did not leave the property, he would be going inside to secure a gun and make him leave. Bromley, intoxicated and in a state of excitement, spoke up and said: "Don't bring out the gun Jim, there is no need of shooting anyone." Bromley then ran across the road and grabbed a piece of fence rail that was lying in the ditch. Old William Phalen continued to tell Bromley to stay off of his property and leave his family in peace.

Phalen, an aged man who had difficulty walking, then proceeded to his front porch. Due to his infirmity, he was unable to move very fast. Bromley returned to the Phalen yard with the fence post in his hands. As Phalen turned his head to attempt to climb the steps to his residence, Bromley brought up the post in a swinging motion and struck the old man in the back of the head. Phalen immediately fell where he had stood. Bromley then began to strike the now prone Phalen about the head while his son attempted to thwart the assault. James Phalen kneeled beside his wounded father and asked for help. His neighbor, who heard the loud screaming that preceded the altercation, then appeared and offered to go secure Sheriff Oyster, who was at the Oyster Hotel in Horton. The Donovans helped the young Phalen carry his father into the house and placed him on the sofa. James Phalen examined his father and found his face and head heavily bruised. His father was still breathing but had lost consciousness. James headed out towards Centerville to find a doctor, and when he arrived in Earleyville, he stopped at Dr. James Earley's residence and told him of the affair. Dr. Earley started towards the Phalen residence. James then proceeded to Centreville and found Doctor Straessley, who accompanied him back to his residence. Both doctors attended to the wounded Phalen the remainder of the night and into the next morning. They found that Phalen had a swelling of the brain and could not relieve the pressure. Phalen lingered on until six in the morning before he expired from a convulsion. Pressure on the brain, due to a blow from the wooden fence rail was the cause of death.

Sheriff Oyster was notified during this period, and he went to the scene of the conflict and arrested Dennis and James Donovan and John Bromley and brought them to the Elk County Jail. William Bromley already had made his escape and could not be located. Esquire Peter Thompson impaneled a coroner's jury, and a post mortem examination was held by Drs. T. S. Harley and James Early, who found that the skull had been fractured in nine different places. The verdict of the coroner's jury was "That William Phalen came to his death by one or more blows inflicted on the skull, producing compression of the brain, from which caused he died. The said blow or blows were given by the hands of one William Bromley. We also say that James Donovan, Dennis Donovan, and John Bromley were accessories to the death of the said William Phalen."

On the following Monday evening, Dennis and James Donovan and John Bromley were taken out of their jail cells and appeared before Judge Vincent, on a writ of habeas corpus, for trial, which resulted in James Donovan and John Bromley being admitted to bail in the sum of $300 each. Dennis Donovan was committed to jail to await his trial at the August term of Court.

The manhunt for William Bromley continued for many months. The Elk County Commissioners offered a $500 reward for the capture of Bromley, but his whereabouts were never known. Reports were printed in the paper that he was captured in New Jersey, but these proved to be untrue. The trial of

Dennis Donovan was delayed until the January 1874 term of Court, in hopes that Bromley would be captured and could be put on trial at the same time as Donovan.

The trial of Dennis Donovan on the charge of being an accessory to the murder of William Phalen commenced on January 22nd, 1874, in the Ridgway Court House. The jury impaneled consisted of Joseph Robinson, Alex Mayhood, Jr., Samuel Vasbinder, Cornelius Whalen, J. H. Meffert, E. H. Dixon, Joseph Riley, Myron Raught, Thomas McKean, William James, John Meyers, and O. B. Fitch.

It came out in the trial that William Bromley had married Dennis Donovan's sister and that they were brothers-in-law. It was also noted that the deceased, William Phalen, had filed charges against William Bromley for stealing some of his sheep. This caused considerable bad blood between Bromley and Phalen before the argument at the Democratic convention. Young Phalen described the argument and subsequent altercation that took place at the meeting and their house. He described Dennis Donovan as the man who first accosted his father and who held him, while William Bromley went and grabbed a fence post which he then hit old Phalen on the head with. Dennis Donovan, John Bromley and James Donovan all testified that they did not strike the old man Phalen and that they did not see William Bromley do it either. Many prominent witnesses were brought in to testify that Dennis Donovan was a man of good caricature. The jury then took the case into consideration and found Dennis Donovan guilty of being an accessory to murder, and he was sentenced to one year and two months imprisonment in the Western Penitentiary. Donovan filed an appeal immediately, and this was denied. Donovan also filed for a pardon to the State Board of Pardons which was denied on November 26th, 1874.

The true murderer of William Phalen, William Bromley, was never captured despite a country-wide manhunt. Perhaps he headed out west with a wagon train or changed his name and remained in Pennsylvania. Whatever his fate, he never answered for his crime and Dennis Donovan took the rap. Joseph Windfelder won the Democratic Party nomination for treasurer and went on to beat the Republican candidate.

The Oyster Hotel at Hellen is a new building, very spacious, finished in modern style and elegantly furnished. We have no hesitation in recomending it to the public. D. C. Oyster is the proprietor.

An announcement from *The Elk County Advocate* of 1870 when the Oyster Hotel was first built in Horton Township.

LAST Friday evening, the Oyster Hotel at Hellen, this county, was burned to the ground. The fire started in an unused room, in the third story and cannot be accounted for. The loss on house and furniture is $13,000, Insurance $5,000.

An article from *The Elk County Advocate* of November 1874, announcing the demise of the Oyster Hotel.

A Father's Revenge

The Bonghi residence and store today.

On March 7th, 1927, Mr. and Mrs. John Bonghi of Ridgway traveled to Crenshaw to attend the funeral of a friend. The Bonghi's owned a small store, located on Front Street in Ridgway and although this was not their main source of income, they could not afford to be out of town without it operating. They decided to leave their thirteen-year-old daughter Susie in charge of running the store and waiting on customers. To be sure that she could handle the job, Mr. Bonghi asked his good friend, Dominic Fiaschetti, to stop in and help his young daughter with any problems that may arise. Fiaschetti, thirty-nine years old, and single, assured Bonghi that he would look after the young Susie and make sure she was safe and sound.

Susie Bonghi opened the store at eight in the morning on March 7th and had very few customers for this Monday. Dominic Fiaschetti arrived around nine in the morning, and after greeting Susie and asking her if she needed any help, he went into the back of the store into the storage room. Fiaschetti called out to Susie to come into the storage room to give him a hand moving a box. Susie came into the room, and Fiaschetti pointed to a box high up on a shelf and asked her to reach up and get it for him while he held her up. Susie did as she was told and when Fiaschetti held her up, he began to molest her. While she was helplessly holding the box, Fiaschetti continued to molest little Susie for a period of time, and Susie remained quiet throughout. Fiaschetti finally let her go and she immediately went to the front of the store and avoided him for the rest of the time he was in the store. Fiaschetti finally left the store after an hour and did not return that day

The Bonghi's returned from Crenshaw in the early evening hours of Monday and found their daughter had already closed the store. Susie was especially quiet throughout the evening and answered her parent's queries with one-word responses. Her parents did not think anything of this behavior and the family retired for the evening. In the following weeks, Susie became more and more withdrawn, but her parents thought this was probably due to her becoming a woman and going through adolescence. Mrs. Bonghi did notice that whenever Fiaschetti's name was brought up, Susie left the room.

On Monday, March 28th, 1927, Mrs. Bonghi was preparing to visit a sick relative in the Elk County General Hospital. Mr. Bonghi had made arrangements for his friend Dominic

Fiaschetti to give his wife and daughter a ride to the hospital, while he stayed back to operate the store. When Mrs. Bonghi mentioned to Susie that Fiaschetti would be picking them up at six in the evening, Susie flatly refused to accompany her. When questioned further, Susie told her mother of what Fiaschetti had done to her earlier in March, when her parents had traveled to Crenshaw. Mrs. Bonghi did not at that moment tell her husband what little Susie had told her. Mr. Fiaschetti arrived at six and entered the store to pick up the Bonghi women. Mr. Bonghi greeted him and called for his wife and daughter. Mrs. Bonghi and Susie entered the room, and Susie refused amid sobs to go with Fiaschetti and at her mother's goading, she told her father, in front of Fiaschetti, what Fiaschetti had done to her when they were in Crenshaw. Mr. Bonghi, stunned by the revelation coming from his daughter, seized a .38 caliber revolver and shot point blank at Fiaschetti who was trying to deny that anything happened. Two of the bullets struck Fiaschetti in the arm, and when Fiaschetti turned to run, a third bullet hit his back and exited through his stomach. A fourth shot hit the ceiling. A neighbor, Frank Cuneo, heard the shooting and quickly entered the store. He saw what had happened and immediately called the police and the ambulance for the injured Fiaschetti. Chief of Police David Lobaugh arrived first and inquired what had happened. Mrs. Bonghi stated that she had shot Fiaschetti because of what he had done to her daughter. Chief Lobaugh did not believe her and readily saw that Mrs. Bonghi could not even hold a pistol properly, much less fire three shots at Fiaschetti. Lobaugh placed Mr. Bonghi under arrest. The ambulance then arrived and transported Fiaschetti to the Elk County General Hospital.

Fiaschetti was rushed into surgery at the hospital, as his intestines were protruding out of his stomach. Dr. Flynn performed the surgery and described the prognosis as promising, but still critical. District Attorney Straub interviewed Fiaschetti, and he denied ever molesting the young Bonghi girl. Fiaschetti said that Mr. Bonghi was the one that shot him, however, when he fell as a result of the shooting, he said Mrs. Bonghi had come up to his head with the gun and wanted to shoot him again. Fiaschetti said that Mr. Bonghi persuaded her to put the weapon down and to leave Fiaschetti as he was. Fiaschetti was employed as a laborer at the Brickyard and was single. Fiaschetti was given a fighting chance at life, but the chances seemed to be against recovery due to the damage done to his intestines. Eventually, peritonitis, or infection of the intestines, set in and Mr. Fiaschetti expired on Tuesday, April 5th, at five in the afternoon, five days after the shooting. His death was not an easy death, as he was in constant pain due to the infection that had enveloped his innards. The funeral for Fiaschetti was held on Friday morning, April 8th, at Saint Leo's Catholic Church in Ridgway and burial followed at the Saint Leo's Cemetery on Montmorenci.

John Bonghi was meanwhile taken in front of Justice Conser on Tuesday morning, where bail was set at $10,000. Over half a dozen friends of Bonghi put up the bail, and he was released to await further charges should Fiaschetti die from his injuries. Bonghi had developed a large amount of sympathy from the community and his friends. Bonghi was employed long term with the Pennsylvania Railroad, while his wife ran the Bonghi Store.

A coroner's inquest was held on Wednesday, April 6th, 1927, the day after Fiaschetti expired. Dr. A. C. Luhr impaneled a jury consisting of Daniel Nolph, Oscar Rickard, W. S. McVey, John Nangle, Ernest Bogert, and H. H. Wensel all of Ridgway. After hearing the testimony of Dr. J. G. Flynn, Frank Cuneo and Arthur Watson, the jury rendered: "From the evidence before us we find Dominick Fiaschetti came to his death by gunshot wounds at the hands of Mr. and Mrs. John Bonghi. We, the jury, recommend that Mr. and Mrs. John Bonghi be held for Grand Jury Action." Warrants were then issued for both Mr. and Mrs. Bonghi. Mr. Bonghi was allowed to remain at liberty on his $10,000 bond. Mrs. Bonghi, who had given birth to a child about a week prior, was bedridden at home and her condition would not permit removal to the county jail. During the hearing, it came out that while Fiaschetti was in the hospital, he charged that Mrs. Bonghi wanted to shoot him in the head as he lay prostrate on the floor from his wounds. This was the reason the coroner's jury indicted Mrs. Bonghi.

The Bonghi's remained free throughout the rest of 1927. The trial was set for the January 1928 term of court, when Mr. Bonghi entered into a plea agreement with District Attorney Straub, in which he would plead guilty to the voluntary manslaughter of Dominic Fiaschetti in return for no jail time and that the charges against his wife would be dropped. At Mr. Bonghi's sentencing on Thursday, January 12th, 1928, Judge Baird, upon the recommendations of both Attorney F. W. McFarlin and District Attorney Straub for leniency, Bonghi was given parole for three years and ordered to pay the costs of prosecution and a fine in the amount of $500.

Wassa Matt?

Galeazzo's tombstone in the Holy Rosary
Catholic Cemetery.

On May 15th, 1923, Frank Galeazzo was sitting in front of his
store, which was located on Railroad Street in Johnsonburg and
located directly behind the rail road station. Galeazzo was

talking with his friend and neighbor, Frank Torchia, on this warm spring evening. As it was close to ten o'clock in the evening, the street was quite dark except for the lights still burning in Galeazzo's store. As the two friends talked, Torchia said he saw a man coming along the fence from the direction of Grant Street. As it was someone Torchia did not know, he did not pay much attention to him. The unknown man walked right up to the front of the Galeazzo store and put his right hand on the side of the store and with his left hand, he produced a revolver. He was about eighteen inches from Galeazzo and began firing the weapon into Galeazzo's torso. He fired three shots rather quickly and ran away as soon as he was done shooting. Torchia immediately picked up his wounded friend Galeazzo and took him into the store where he telephoned for the police and a doctor. The only words that Galeazzo said, according to Torchia, were "Frank, he shot me." Johnsonburg Police Officer James Wright was the first authority on the scene, quickly followed by the Feronti Taxi, which transported both Galeazzo and Torchia to the Elk County General Hospital.

Galeazzo, admitted to the hospital with a gun wound to the stomach, lingered on until Sunday, May 20th, 1927, when he succumbed to peritonitis which was common when the intestines were ruptured from a gunshot. Galeazzo had been a resident of Johnsonburg for more than twenty-five years and was a highly respected merchant. He was survived by a wife Mary, and two children. Funeral services were held on Wednesday Morning, May the 23rd from the Holy Rosary Church, and were attended by a large crowd of mourners accompanied by numerous floral tributes. Burial took place at the Wardvale Cemetery in Johnsonburg. Galeazzo was forty-six years old.

Elk County Coroner Luhr conducted an inquest on the remains of Frank Galeazzo on Monday afternoon, the 21st of May, at the Ubel Funeral Home in Johnsonburg. The jury impaneled was composed of Alva Gregory, E. L. Brennan, Alex Basinger, Francis Straessley, George Long and M. E. Ware. Dr. Luhr told the jury that the investigation of the injuries on Galeazzo's body showed a wound on the left arm that shattered the bone, and a wound in the abdomen that perforated the bowel, death resulting from peritonitis.

Frank Torchia, of Johnsonburg, who formerly conducted a barber shop on Railroad Street, close to the Galeazzo store, was the only witness heard. He said he was a close personal friend of Galeazzo, and often visited the latter's store. Torchia said it was a common occurrence for them to sit in front of Galeazzo's store and talk.

Torchia's story was that he was talking with Galeazzo in front of his store when he observed a man coming along the fence from the direction of Grant Street, about twenty-five feet away. Torchia said the man wore a brown raincoat and a brown hat. The unknown man put his right arm on the side of the Galeazzo store, and with his left hand he produced a pistol and shot Galeazzo. The man then ran away as soon as the shots were fired. Torchia said he picked up Galeazzo and took him inside the store where he called the authorities. According to Torchia, the only words said were "Frank, he shot me!" Torchia did say that immediately before the shooting, he and Galeazzo and a traveling man were in the store waiting until the next train arrived. When the train arrived, the traveling man went out to get on the train to go to Ridgway. Galeazzo and Torchia followed him out of the store to see him off, and this was when they sat outside talking and when the unknown assailant appeared.

Dr. Luhr also told the jury that Galeazzo did not make any death bed confessions when he was in the hospital. The jury then returned the following verdict: "We, the jury, find that Frank Galeazzo came to his death from a gunshot wound inflicted by a person unknown to the jury."

The investigation into the murder of Frank Galeazzo began immediately after the wounded man was transported to the hospital. What was kept secret, was the fact that the Elk County Authorities were aided in this investigation by Buffalo, New York Detective Sergeant John Smaldino, who specialized in Black Hand crimes. A connection between the slaying of Galeazzo and the Black Hand in Johnsonburg and Buffalo was discovered, and Smaldino was recruited to assist. What Smaldino uncovered would be explosive.

Frank Torchia was arrested on Thursday, July 19th, 1923 and charged with being an accessory before the fact, in the murder of Frank Galeazzo. If Torchia was an accessory, he was considered equally guilty as the man who fired the shots. Torchia was taken to the Elk County Jail where a hearing was held in the corridor. Justice of the Peace, C. C. Consor presided. Detective Smaldino, who had worked the case quietly since the shooting occurred, produced several witnesses that contradicted Torchia's version of events.

Charles Maloney, a reputable young man from Johnsonburg, was called to give his testimony. Maloney said that on the night of the shooting, he was conversing with Night Policeman James Wright and Patsy Feronti on the railroad station platform at the time the Pennsy train was due at the depot. He said he heard three shots out of the blue. Officer Wright determined that they were not made by the train. Meanwhile, Feronti and Malone got into Feronti's taxicab and drove rapidly around in front of the train to the intersection of Grant and Railroad Street, on the other side of the railroad tracks. Maloney left the car and ran towards the place from which the three reports were heard. When about one hundred and fifty feet from the store of Frank Galeazzo, he met a man hurrying in the opposite direction. Both halted abruptly and then the short, squat man asked Maloney, "Wassa Matt?' Wassa Matt'? Maloney said he replied: "How in the hell do I know" and continued towards the store. Here he found Frank Galeazzo, sitting in a chair on the porch of the building and nearby stood Frank Monea, a Johnsonburg man.

Maloney alleged that he remained there a couple of minutes and noticed the man, whom he passed, was still standing where he had halted. Maloney inquired of someone, whom he did not remember, "Who is that standing over there?" "Why that's Frank Torchia," was the reply. The witness was certain of his identification, saying that the man's build, clothing, and mannerisms were the same as that of the defendant.

Maloney testified that a short time afterward, Torchia was seen in the store where Galeazzo had been removed too. When Torchia was asked what the murderer, the man who fired the shots, looked like, he said that he wore a cap and a coat just like Maloney's, pointing towards him.

Torchia's statement after the shooting says that he arranged for the transportation of Galeazzo to the Ridgway hospital, accompanied him and assisted the nurses at the hospital in removing his clothes. Torchia also stated that he never left the side of Galeazzo and it was he who moved Galeazzo into the store after the shooting.

Justice Consor then ruled that Torchia be held on murder charges until a habeas corpus proceeding could be held at the end of July. The habeas corpus hearing would determine whether to file charges against Torchia formally and would also decide then, if and what amount of bail would be allowed.

After the hearing in the jail, a lively conversation took place between Detective Smaldino and Torchia. The defendant said that he could get a "thousand" witnesses to prove that he had not left Galeazzo for a second after the shooting. Smaldino replied "Every witness you get will go behind bars there with you. We're going to get you and every one of your dirty gang!" Smaldino then told the local reporters that he has been working under the district attorney's office almost from the beginning. He said that he was determined to get to the bottom of this crime and said that the convincing testimony introduced at the hearing was but a small part of that which has been unearthed.

The habeas corpus hearing for Frank Torchia was held on Saturday, July the 30th, in Ridgway in front of Judge Baird. F. W. McFarlin, District Attorney, represented the Commonwealth, while D. J. Driscoll represented the defendant. The object of the proceedings was to fix bail for the prisoner, if any would be allowed, or to discharge the defendant as the Court deemed proper. It was up to the Commonwealth to produce as much evidence as deemed necessary to allow the charges to be sustained.

The first witness called was young John Galeazzo, son of the murdered man. The boy cried as he went to the stand, talked very low and his evidence seemed to have only a very small bearing on the question at issue.

The chief witness for the Commonwealth was Charles Maloney, of Johnsonburg, who took the stand next. Maloney swore to have seen Torchia hurrying down Railroad Street right after the shooting and greeting him. Maloney also swore that he did not see who carried Galeazzo into the store after the shooting, that he never saw Torchia before that night, and that he did not know who told him the man's name was Torchia. He stuck to his story that the man he first passed about eighty-five feet from the scene of the crime was Torchia and that the next time he saw Torchia, was in the store after Galeazzo had been carried in.

D. R. Lobaugh, Chief of Police of Ridgway, told of his arrest of Torchia at the hospital, and he identified a statement purporting to have been made, signed and sworn to by Torchia in the Ridgway Jail. The statement claimed Torchia had not left Galeazzo's side after the shooting. The Commonwealth's contention, by the testimony of Maloney, was that Torchia, after the shooting, had been seen, as the witness Maloney claimed, eighty-five feet from the scene. The Commonwealth also pointed out that Maloney saw no-one else in Railroad Street, and that the "stranger" who shot Galeazzo was none other than Frank Torchia.

The Commonwealth then rested, and Attorney Driscoll asked Judge Baird to dismiss the charges against his client, Torchia, as they were not sufficient to hold him. Judge Baird questioned District Attorney McFarlin as to whether there was any other evidence that he could present. McFarlin stated they did not, and with that, the Judge ruled that Torchia be discharged as the evidence presented by the Commonwealth was insufficient to hold Torchia on the murder charge. In the Judge's opinion, it would be a waste of public money to hold the prisoner for this action. Charges against Torchia were then dismissed, and he left the Court a free man, never to be charged with the murder of Frank Galeazzo.

Detective Smaldino was furious after the charges were dismissed. No other suspect was ever produced in this case, and the Commonwealth believed that the guilty party was arrested and charged, they just did not have enough evidence to prosecute. Was there a mysterious man who did the shooting? That was never to be known. Even if the shooter did escape, Torchia and indeed Galeazzo knew much more than what they said. The fact that Galeazzo never talked about what had happened also furthers the case that he knew the assailant and more than likely the assailant was Torchia. The unusual addition of Buffalo New York Detective Smaldino to the case was also quite peculiar. The Black Hand operated throughout Elk County, specifically Johnsonburg and Ridgway, from before the turn of the century, up to and including the later days of the 20th century.

Frank Galeazzo's death certificate.

The Saga of Frederick Kress Rockwell

Frederick Kress Rockwell

On January 3rd, 1897, an old hunter & trapper by the name of "Boney" DeRock was out on Mill Creek, in Jones Township,

Elk County, looking after some wild cat traps he had set. He soon came upon the area where Gore & Murphy, a lumber company, had abandoned an earlier operation and had left a wooden blacksmith shop standing. Boney noticed that the wooden structure had recently burned to the ground. Boney decided to look through the remains of the cabin for some scrap-iron for a sled he was making. As he picked through the ash, he noticed a burnt carcass within the embers. He at first believed the carcass to have been some sort of animal, that a hunting party had brought into the forest and which had burned up when they set fire to the shanty. When Boney made a closer inspection, however, he was startled at finding that the remains were those of a man. DeRock did not touch the remains and instead headed directly to the Highland Township Justice of the Peace to report his gruesome find. The Justice of the Peace hastily formed a coroner's jury, who soon after met at the burned-out cabin. The jury ruled that the remains, devoid of any identification, were those of unknown man and that they had come to their death at the hands of some unknown person. They made this determination after finding that the back of the skull of the deceased suffered obvious trauma. The unknown body was buried in the Highland Corners Cemetery.

The case of the unknown murder victim was turned over to the authorities at Elk County for further investigation. The first theory was that the deceased was a man named Burns, who had disappeared from the town of Kane, in McKean County, which was situated about five miles from the scene of the crime. This theory was quickly discounted. The next scenario was that the body was from some unknown hunter, who had become under the influence of liquor while bunking in the old shanty overnight and had accidentally set fire to the shanty and had perished in the ruins. As no hunter was reported missing, this scenario too was discounted. Elk County District Attorney Fred H. Ely then became interested in the case of the unsolved murder and in conjunction with County Detective Mack Kime, started a quiet investigation of the affair.

Elk County authorities were aware of a series of burglaries which had been taking place in the upper reaches of Elk County, McKean County, and Forest County. The bands of outlaws had recently been captured in Forest County and were jailed at the Tionesta lockup. The arrested group included one Frederick K. Rockwell, John Newell, Robert Rockwell, and Mrs. Annie Haines. They all had been charged with burglary and receiving stolen goods. The authorities in all three counties had the "gang" in their list of suspects for the recent crimes and were anxious to interrogate them. The "ringleader," Mr. Louis Haines, was, however, missing when the group was captured. The missing leader raised the eyebrows of the Elk County Authorities, and they decided to go to Tionesta to question the suspects as to the whereabouts of Mr. Haines. What developed from the interrogations would be one of the most famous and most heart-wrenching murder cases to ever take place in Elk County.

Frederick Kress Rockwell was born on August 25th, 1871 in East Brady, Clarion County. His early life was normal, until his father, in an argument over a girl in the neighborhood, left the family and was reported to have moved to Denver, Colorado and was never heard from again. Frederick's life then became one of uncertainty, and he was often moved from place to place, wherever his mother chose to live. His mother eventually gave Frederick and his brother Robert, and sister Lina to a group called the Overseers of the Poor, where they remained for quite some time. The children were then taken to a private asylum, located at Smethport, in McKean County. All three children were separated at this time, with the younger son Robert being sent to Oswayo in Potter County. Frederick "escaped" from these accommodations in his teen years and began to attempt to support himself by whatever means necessary. Through years of moving around in an attempt to make a living, Frederick was finally able to reconnect with his mother and brother, and they all ended up in Highland, Elk County. Frederick at first lived with his mother and her new husband, Boney DeRock. After a falling out with his mother, Frederick built his own shanty and made his living as a bark peeler at the various lumber operations that existed in the area. Rockwell's life would change forever when he returned to his shack on October 16th, 1896 and found it occupied by strangers. Up until this time, Rockwell had been known to have a good reputation as a hard and honest worker.

The "group" of people who had squatted in Rockwell's shack included Mr. Louis Haines, his wife Annie, their four children, Mrs. Haines brother, John Newell and Mrs. Haines mother, Mrs. Phoebe Newell. Rockwell was both delighted and annoyed by these uninvited guests. Rockwell also found that Annie, Louis's wife, would not leave him alone. As the young Rockwell was naïve in the ways of women and romance, he did not understand this constant attention he was receiving from Annie. As his shack was quite small, Annie and the children moved in with Rockwell's aunt who lived next door. After a short time, Louis Haines exclaimed he had to find work and left the area in search of pay. Rockwell was planning a hunting expedition in the Adirondack Mountains in New York at this time. He visited Annie at his Aunt's house and asked her if she would watch over his shack while he was gone and if he could leave his possessions with her until he returned. Rockwell offered the use of his shack while he was on his hunting expedition. Annie began the timeless art of seduction to keep Rockwell from leaving the area.

Annie agreed to watch over his shack and possessions, but also said she would need help that weekend to move their possessions into his shack. After he had helped the Haines family move into his shack, a fire erupted during the night, which torched the entire shack and left all of them homeless. Rockwell lost everything in the fire, including his rifle and hunting dog which he planned to take to the Adirondacks. This fire was to have the most unforeseen circumstances. The entire group then moved into Rockwell's aunt's house in Highland. Once again, a wood fire destroyed that abode and the group were again homeless and lost all of their possessions. House fires were common in those days. The group then went to Rockwell's uncle's home. While residing there, Mr. Haines reappeared from working, and Mrs. Haines would not speak to him. She blamed her husband for causing the fire at both of the previous residences. She began to confide much more in young Rockwell and during this time she first kissed him on the lips while sharing her story of an unhappy marriage with Mr. Haines. Annie began to follow Rockwell relentlessly when he was at the house and kept saying "What will I do with this family I've got?" "I don't know what to do?" "I have nobody to care for me, but I will have him arrested." "I believe he burned the house down." Rockwell believed she was making a proposition; that if she divorced her husband or had him arrested would Rockwell marry her? Rockwell finally said to Annie, "will you marry me? Annie responded "Yes! I'll marry you as soon as anybody else." The couple then dropped the subject, until she either divorced her husband or had him arrested. Annie had her mother, Phoebe, try to get her husband arrested, but this did not happen. Annie continued to romance Rockwell every moment she could when others were not around.

During October 1896, Rockwell traveled throughout Elk and McKean counties in search of employment. He was mostly unsuccessful and returned once again to his Aunt's residence and the Haines family. The whole group was now desperate for money, and they began to scheme on how they could get some. Rockwell suggested they steal a horse and sell it for the needed funds. Mr. Haines said that was his style, but he suggested they break into some stores to get essential supplies and whatever else was available. They all agreed that this was the quickest and easiest way to solve their problems.

The group, consisting of Rockwell, Haines, and Newell, chose the store at Duhring as their first target, as John Newell had previously worked there and was familiar with the building. When they arrived at the store, they found it was still occupied, and they could not break in without being caught. They decided to go a quarter of a mile down the road to another store, and finding this one closed, were able to remove a pane of glass and open the door. Haines filled his pockets with crackers while Rockwell chose shoes and clothes for the woman and children. When they left, Haines had only secured a few medicine bottles and tobacco, along with the crackers. This caused Rockwell to resent Haines as he was only looking out for himself. The Duhring store robbery was the first of what became an almost nightly occurrence, with the gang raiding store after store and farm after farm. Mrs. Haines rejoiced every time the trio came back with booty and wrapped her arms around Rockwell's neck and gave him many kisses. She would continue hugging him and calling him her "darling" and her "pet" and her "little man" and that she was going to have him one day. Rockwell continued to delight Annie by bringing home some chickens he pilfered from one man's farm and even a beehive from another when Annie asked for something sweet.

Haines and Rockwell then went to Russell City and broke into a large store. They carried out over $75 worth of goods, in small increments and realized they would be unable to carry it all back to their house. They hauled the loot up into the woods and hid most of the goods. They decided they would need to steal a horse and buggy to transport the goods. They planned to steal a horse and buggy off of the streets of Kane, but when they arrived in Kane, they decided it would be too risky. They then went towards the Highland Road, to the Johnson farm, and Haines went up to the barn, went inside, struck up a match and inspected the stable. Haines did not find a buggy or horse to his liking, and the gang went to the next farm. They saw a buggy in the back of the house which they moved to the road and Haines went into the barn and stole the horse. They were now on wheels, and all of them headed back towards Russell City to pick up their loot. The provisions lasted for a while, but in December of 1896, supplies were getting low, and Haines and Rockwell knew they would have to do something to survive the winter months.

Each time Haines and Rockwell returned to their house after a nighttime raid, not only would Haines's wife shower Rockwell with affection, but her mother, old Mrs. Newell, would pull him aside and beg him to kill Haines in some way. She suggested he could take Haines to some mill pond and tie a rock around his neck and throw him in or throw him off some railroad bridge to his death. Whenever Mrs. Newell was behind Haines, she would make pretend motions like she was stabbing him with a knife. Rockwell was also under pressure from Mrs. Haines to get rid of her husband once and for all, or she would have nothing further to do with Rockwell. He told Mrs. Haines that the deed would be done soon, and they would be together forever. Rockwell devised plans to kill Haines at some distant location and burn his body so as the murder would not be detected. He went out with Haines on the morning of December the 17th, and after their usual looting, they began to return home. Rockwell had told Mrs. Haines that he would stab her husband and set him on fire on this trip, but he could not bring himself to do it, and Mrs. Haines was surprised to see her husband arrive back to the house still alive. She pestered Rockwell with questions of "why didn't you do that?" and "Why did you bring him back home?" She also withheld her usual affectionate hug and kisses to punish Rockwell.

On the morning of the 20th of December 1896, Mrs. Haines stood in the doorway of the bedroom where Rockwell slept and said to him: "Fred Rockwell, tomorrow when you go away with Lou Haines, don't you bring him back. If you do, you don't need to come back here, for I won't have anything to do with you!" Rockwell, in love with this woman, and not wanting to lose her affections, decided that the 21st of December would be the day he would rid Mrs. Haines of her burden and also gain the woman of his desires.

Haines was murdered at the head end of Mill Creek, located along the Brush Hollow trailhead off of present-day Route 948 towards Highland.

On the morning of December 21st, 1896, Haines and Rockwell left the house and were on a mission to either find a place to plunder or find a job. They walked along Coon Run Road in Highland and passed the old Mr. Riley farm (from the first volume), and saw he had a large hog hanging that he had butchered. They both remarked that this would be a good place to get pork in the future. Rockwell then told Haines that they should head towards Mill Creek as he had heard they were hiring in a lumber camp there. They walked along the Highland Road, and when they came to Brush Hollow, Rockwell led Haines up the hollow towards the old Gore & Murphy camp number five. As they reached the head end of Mill Creek, they came upon the old blacksmith shop. Rockwell complained of having cold feet and suggested they go into the shanty to start a fire and warm themselves. Haines drew a large buck knife and began to make wood shavings to start the fire, while Rockwell secured a thick bar of iron and began ripping boards off of the wall to feed the fire. As Haines kneeled over the fire, Rockwell approached him from behind with the metal bar. He raised the bar several times to swing, but each time he hesitated. After thinking about what Mrs. Haines had told him about having nothing to do with him if he did not kill her husband, he finally raised the bar and struck Haines squarely in the back of the head. Haines raised his head and attempted to stand up when Rockwell hit him again. Haines did not move after the second blow. Rockwell immediately felt remorse and did not know what to do. He devised a plan to burn the shack along with the body, to hide any evidence of his evil deed. He piled the boards he had loosened from the walls over Haines's body and struck a match to ignite the fire. Before he stepped out of the shack, he remembered what John Newell had told him that morning, that when he killed Haines, he should bring his boots back as proof he was dead. Rockwell pulled the boots off of the body and put them on. He also took off Haines's hat and put it into his pocket as further proof of his deed. He then went outside and watched the fire burn, until the roof of the cabin caved in. He thought he had committed the perfect murder until the old trapper Boney DeRock discovered his crime early in January. As it was late in the evening, Rockwell went to the nearby abandoned Holland House and made a fire in the stove and slept through the night.

Early the next morning, Rockwell left for home and went by way of Highland Corners through Russell City, and he was home just before daylight. He told everyone of what had happened and trusted they would never betray the story. Mrs. Haines asked to see her husband's boots as proof, and when she saw them, she rejoiced. After that night, Rockwell slept with Mrs. Haines every night up to, and including the night they were all finally arrested for breaking into the Songer's house in Forest County. The gang had been in the eye of the authorities in three counties, and although their names were known, the police had been unable to find their hideout and had not been able to catch them in the act. While the gang was inside the uninhabited Songer house, they had decided to stay the night. A neighbor had noticed lights inside the large house and had notified the authorities of the break-in. When law enforcement had arrived, they found the gang sleeping in the beds and arrested Frederick Rockwell, his brother Robert Rockwell, John Newell and Annie Haines. The gang was taken to the jail in Tionesta, and a report was sent out to local law enforcement in Elk and McKean counties that the gang was finally captured. The Elk County Authorities were quite interested in this arrest and noticed right away that the ringleader, Louis Haines, was not among those arrested. A fact that did not go unnoticed and a fact that would prove to be fatal to Frederick Rockwell.

The Elk County Authorities traveled to the Tionesta Jail to interview the detainees and elicited enough information from the mouths of John Newell and Annie Haines to convince them that they were on the right track. They were convinced that the body found at Mill Creek was Louis Haines and that a great crime was about to be solved. The old Mrs. Phoebe Newell was also interviewed, and she confirmed that the body found at Mill Creek was indeed her son-in-law Louis Haines, and she proceeded to tell the authorities the whole story of the murder as relayed to her by Frederick Rockwell. District Attorney Ely informed Elk County Coroner Mullhaupt of their investigation, and Mullhaupt impaneled a coroner's jury at Mike Costello's Hotel (later the Highland Hotel) in short order. Mullhaupt had the remains of Haines, previously buried in the Highland Cemetery, exhumed and a second autopsy was performed. The jury heard the testimony of Mrs. Phoebe Haines, Boney DeRock and Mrs. S. E. DeRock. The next day the jury traveled to the Tionesta Jail and received the testimony of Robert Rockwell, Mrs. Annie Haines, and John Newell. They also heard testimony from Frederick Rockwell; this testimony would later cause a mistrial due to the way it was elicited. The jury returned a verdict that "Louis Haines had come to his death on December 21st, 1896, by the hands of Frederick Rockwell" and a warrant was issued charging Rockwell with first-degree murder in Elk County. Louis Haines' body was returned to his former burial place in the Highland Cemetery.

At the Spring Term of the Forest County Court, Rockwell plead guilty to the charge of burglary, and the sentence was suspended by Judge Charles Noye of Warren County, pending his trial for the greater crime of murder in Elk County.

Rockwell was transported to the Elk County Jail at the end of February 1897 and employed Ernest J. Wimmer as his defense attorney. Rockwell's first trial took place on April 5th, 1897, in the Elk County Courthouse. The presiding Judge was C. A. Mayer, and the associate Judges were John R. Kime of Ridgway and Michael Cashman of Saint Marys. District Attorney Fred Ely of Ridgway represented the Commonwealth. The Commonwealth presented over twenty witnesses including Dr.

Mullhaupt, Boney DeRock, Mrs. Phoebe Newell and the star witness, Mrs. Annie Haines. They all testified with their general knowledge of the case, with the old Mrs. Newell testifying that it was Rockwell's idea to murder Haines and she denied she ever suggested it. The main witness, Annie, admitted that she had developed a love interest in Rockwell and that she had suggested that if her husband were out of the way, she would marry him. She also said that she did not know if her husband was dead, as she only knew what Rockwell had told her, and had never seen the body herself. Rockwell's testimony to the coroner's jury, given under duress in the Forest County Jail, was also included in the evidence. The defense vigorously attacked the submission of the confession, in which Rockwell had admitted to the killing. The defense's premise was that the body found in Mill Creek was not that of Haines and that Haines was still alive. Wimmer vowed to prove that no one could say with one hundred percent accuracy that the body that now lay in the Highland Cemetery was Louis Haines. After three days of testimony, the case was given to the jury. On Thursday morning, April 8th, the jury returned with a verdict of guilty of murder in the first degree. The penalty for first-degree murder in those days was death by hanging. Rockwell appeared to take the verdict with no emotion, much as he appeared throughout the trial. It was noted that he only showed emotion when the object of his desire, Annie Haines, was present in the courtroom. Attorney Wimmer vowed he would appeal, and Judge Mayer set the appeal argument date in the middle of July. Rockwell was taken back to the jail in chains to await the outcome of his appeal and subsequent sentencing if the appeal was unsuccessful.

On July 16th, Wimmer made a plea for a new trial before Judge Mayer. Wimmer argued for an hour that the confession elicited from his client while he was incarcerated in Forest County violated his civil rights and the introduction of the confession into the previous trial caused an unfair verdict. Wimmer quoted from the Declaration of Rights that no person shall be compelled to give evidence again himself, and this confession was exactly what it was referring too. Wimmer argued that the Elk County Authorities had no jurisdiction in Forest County to hold a coroner's jury and therefore any "evidence," such as the confession, should be deemed inadmissible at the trial. He noted that Rockwell was dragged from his cell in front of the illegally assembled coroner's jury and the authorities directed him to testify, without warning him that he could remain quiet and could request counsel before he spoke. He also noted the authorities also never told Rockwell that whatever he said would be used against him in the court. Judge Mayer took this argument into consideration, with a ruling on a new trial to be announced at a later date.

On September 22nd, a new trial was granted based upon the error of admitting the testimony taken at the coroner's inquest, at Tionesta, at the trial. This marked a win for Rockwell's attorney, and Mr. Wimmer lost no time preparing for the second trial.

The second trial of Frederick Rockwell commenced on Monday, November 15th, 1897, in Ridgway. The selection of a jury took an inordinate amount of time, as many had already formed an opinion due to the newspaper coverage of the first trial. The testimony and witnesses presented were essentially the same as the first trial, with the exception that the confession of Rockwell was not admitted into the evidence. The case went to the jury on Tuesday evening, around six o'clock. The jury retired, and after two hours, they announced they had reached a verdict. At eight o'clock the jury returned to the Court and presented their verdict to Judge Mayer. Guilty of murder in the first degree! The penalty for that conviction was death by hanging. Rockwell, who remained calm throughout the trial, slowly put his head down. He was escorted from the Courthouse and placed in his cell at the Elk County Jail.

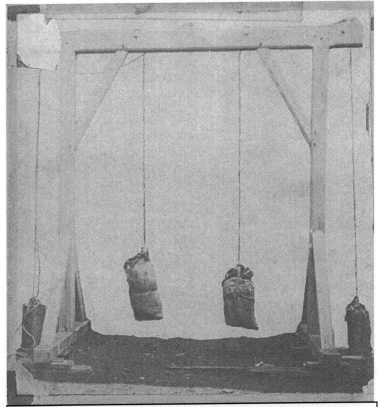

A picture of the gallows constructed for Rockwell and Patsy Banya.
(Photo courtesy of the Elk County Historical Society)

Two days later, Attorney Wimmer asked for another trial for his client. It seemed to many that Rockwell had become more than a client to Wimmer, and this case had become a personal fight for his client. The petition for a new trial was denied, and Frederick K. Rockwell was ordered to stand up in Court for his sentencing. He was asked if he had anything to say as to why a sentence of death should not be imposed upon him. Rockwell answered "nothing." Judge Mayer pronounced the sentence "to be taken from the Jail of Elk County and to be hanged by the neck until he was dead, and may God have mercy upon your soul." The date of execution was set as April 26th, 1898, in Ridgway. Rockwell was to share the gallows with one Patsy Banya, who also had been convicted of first-degree murder.

Wimmer kept on fighting for the life of Rockwell, making a final plea in front of Governor Hastings in Harrisburg on April 18th, 1898. Wimmer said he had proof that Louis Haines was seen alive on December 28th, 1896; seven days after the alleged murder, and therefore the "Newell" faction, which swore away the life of Rockwell, were mistaken when they testified that Haines had been murdered on December 21st, 1896. Governor Hastings declined to issue a reprieve, and Wimmer returned to Ridgway; all hope to stop the execution exhausted.

The day before the execution, Rockwell was baptized into the Catholic Faith by Father Meagher, the Pastor of Saint Leo's Church in Ridgway. He made one request of Father Meagher, that being; for the Father to make sure that all life had left his body before allowing the authorities to bury him. Wimmer met with Rockwell for a seven-hour session, where Rockwell made a full confession and Wimmer recorded the whole story by shorthand notes, which he later published. Rockwell told Wimmer that all of the testimony that was heard in the trial was true, with one exception. Old Mrs. Newell had lied when she said he had suggested killing Haines. He said she and she alone had continuously suggested that he murder her son-in-law. Rockwell also said that all of this had come about because of a woman's false love. Annie drew the sword of false love and struck Rockwell and her husband. His advice was for any young man to run and never consider an affair with a married woman; it could only turn to disaster.

The scaffold for the double hanging of Rockwell and Banya was erected in the corridor of the County Jail, and admission was by ticket only. The weights at the end of the ropes amounted to three hundred and forty-six pounds, and hung three feet eight inches from the floor, with nineteen inches of slack in each rope. Early on the morning of April the 26th, crowds began to arrive at Ridgway, each hoping to attend the execution. However, admission was only given to those who had tickets, and the crowd had to wait outside the corridor, which was hidden by a wall. At twenty-three minutes to eleven, the prisoners, Rockwell and Banya were brought to the gallows. Both carried a crucifix. Father Meagher accompanied Rockwell, while an Italian priest, Father DeVille of Walston, accompanied Patsy Banya. Both men prayed with their clergy and made no final statements. The black veils were then drawn over their heads, and the nooses were adjusted. At eighteen minutes to eleven, Sheriff McMackin cut the rope that held the weights, and the men jerked in space. Rockwell's body gave a few convulsive jerks, and he was suspended for about nineteen minutes before his pulse died out. Rockwell died of strangulation, and his neck was not broken. Rockwell was officially certified as dead by Coroner Mullhaupt, and his body was transported to the St. Leo's Catholic Cemetery for burial. Thus, ended the life and saga of Frederick Kress Rockwell.

Rockwell and Banya were the first and the last public executions that took place in Elk County. He certainly was guilty of first-degree murder, because the murder was premeditated. He only killed Haines because of the love of Mrs. Haines, and while he was certainly naïve, he allowed his emotions and lust to overcome his natural instinct of what was right versus what was wrong. Rockwell was used by Mrs. Haines to rid her of her husband, but Rockwell committed this heinous act. One wonders if Rockwell had not met up with the Newell gang, how his life would have borne out. If he had made the Adirondack hunting trip only a week earlier, he would never have met Annie, and his fate would have been much different.

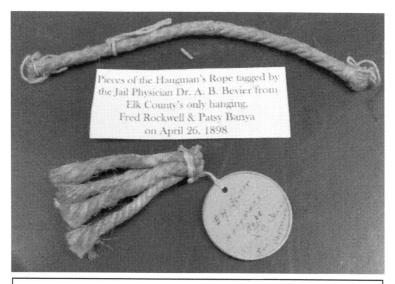

Rope used to hang Rockwell in the Elk County Historical Society Collection.

The Old Eagle Eye from Wilcox

Smith Brother's Store in Wilcox, one of the targets of the West Shore Gang. Now Peterson's Studio.

In the later years of the 1890s, a gang of career criminals was operating along the lines of the P. & E. Rail Road tracks. The gang was known as the "West Shore Gang" and had been accused of many burglaries and armed robberies in towns and villages located throughout Western Pennsylvania. The railroad detectives were following the gang with the assistance of local authorities. Numerous attempts were made to trap the gang in each county, but they remained elusive. In 1899, the group was operating in Clarion County and had robbed a number of stores. While the local authorities were out searching for the gang, they visited the remote shack of a man named Kiser, to see if he had seen any sign of the gang. When the posse entered his cabin, they found the cabin ransacked and Kiser murdered. Kiser was rumored to have hidden a large amount of money in his house, and it appeared the gang had found this out and had killed the old man in the search for his treasure.

Murder charges were added to the other existing charges that the gang had already committed. The gang, who numbered around ten members, now realized that they could be executed for their nefarious behaviors and decided to rob and plunder with reckless abandon. They split up, with part of the gang going to Jefferson County and blowing up a safe at the Brockwayville depot and looting $180. The other members went to Warren County and robbed several stores in Sheffield. Railroad Detective Joy relentlessly pursued the gang. He was fairly successful and arrested five of the gang members near Highland and had them placed in the Elk County Jail. This part of the gang was the one that had committed numerous robberies in Sheffield, and they were on their way to meet up with the rest of the gang. Four members of the gang, however, were able to make their escape from Highland and made their way over the hill to Wilcox.

On June 6th, 1900, at about three o'clock in the morning, the robbers broke into The Smith Brother's large store and stole a large amount of jewelry. The gang then went to the Wilcox House bar and stole cigars and whiskey. The gang then went to the Johnson's Store. Mr. Johnson, who lived upstairs, was awakened by the noise of the burglars. Johnson drove them out of the store with several gunshots, none of which hit their mark. A group of glass plant workers and a telegraph operator were standing outside of the glass plant and observed the burglars and the direction they fled. The alarm was shortly raised with the Sheriff in Elk County and he, along with his deputies, came to Wilcox to set up a posse early in the morning, soon after the robberies. The Sheriff had been given information that the gang was camped out at a place above Wilcox. The location of their camp was about a half a mile behind the present-day cemetery. The gang had found an abandoned hunting camp, and they used this as a headquarters. They were noticed by a local trapper, who saw smoke coming out of the chimney. The posse divided into two parties, with one heading up Dahoga towards Kane. This posse was supposed to circle and head back towards Wilcox. The other group would leave Wilcox and head straight towards the reported encampment. In the Wilcox detachment was an old hunter named Beckwith. As the group proceeded north out of Wilcox, they soon came upon the encampment. Beckwith saw the gang at the same time that the gang saw him. One of the gang fired at him very suddenly at close range, but Beckwith dodged behind a young sapling just in time. Two more shots were fired at him by the robbers before he had time to raise his gun. Beckwith then raised his rifle to his shoulder and taking aim, sent one shot after the hindmost fleeing robber. The bullet proved true in its path and hit the robber just above the eye and literally blew the entire top of his head off. After he fired, he started to shift his position, when his feet caught in a root and he fell just as two more shots passed over his head.

The surviving three members of the gang headed towards Kane with Detective Joy in hot pursuit. They were seen at the "Y" in Kane at an early hour Saturday morning, and Detective Joy shouted to them to hold up their hands and surrender, but one of the men shook a revolver at him and made off into the woods. Joy fired shots at him, but the distance was too far, and they all got away.

Mr. Beckwith was made the hero of the hour at Wilcox, with many wishing he had been given a chance to shoot at all of the robbers. A coroner's jury exonerated him from all blame for shooting the burglar. The body of the slain burglar was identified as one Harry Gordon, by C. M. Castor, described as a traveling man who had stopped in Wilcox on the way to Ridgway. Gordon was one of the prime suspects in the Clarion County murder. The remains of Gordon were buried in the Wilcox Cemetery.

The rest of the gang who escaped was eventually killed in a shootout near Salamanca, New York in the following months. The five members that were imprisoned all drew heavy prison sentences in Warren and Clarion counties. The goods stolen from the Wilcox robberies and many other valuables were found at the abandoned campsite outside of Wilcox, but most of the gold and silver took in the many robberies was never discovered. There is a really good chance that the loot remains buried somewhere between Wilcox and Salamanca, undiscovered to this day.

The view of Wilcox from the cemetery. It was a
half mile behind the cemetery where the gang was
hiding. The one robber that was shot, Harry
Gordon, is buried in this same cemetery.

Go-Devil

Ignac Kordon
Photo courtesy of his granddaughter, Marcia Bleggi.

John Jane, of Rathbun, had taken a hike in the deep woods located in that locale back in early February of 1921. Jane, who worked as a lumberman, walked the entire length of Seeley Hollow and in his search for new timber, he became disoriented. Over the next twenty-five days, Jane would have no idea where he was or how he would get back to his camp. Jane survived in this remote, desolate wilderness using his extensive outdoors skills. Search parties, organized by his fellow lumbermen, had been searching for him without success. The search parties had given up on finding Jane alive, because of the harsh winter weather that blanketed the valley during the winter of 1921. Jane, meanwhile, had somehow traveled many miles back into the woods and was fortunate enough to find an abandoned hunting camp which was stocked with food and had a working wood stove in it. With the food and the fire, Jane was able to withstand the cold weather, and after a break in the weather in early March, he once again took off and was successful in finding his way back to where he started. He was able to follow a small spring that eventually emptied into Seeley Hollow and by following the stream; he ended up on West Creek near where he entered the woods. Jane went to the camp of John Parr, and there was much rejoicing when Jane appeared. Parr, who was a great friend of Jane, immediately organized a party to welcome home Jane and celebrate his escaping death from the cold, harsh wilderness.

That Jane was now safe and sound back in Rathbun caused sensations in Saint Marys. One of Jane's friends, Ignac "James" Kordon was especially happy that Jane was found alive. Ignac, in company with his friends John Glatz and Tony Zora, set out from Saint Marys to visit with Jane at the camp of John Parr in Rathbun. The celebration lasted all day long and consisted of fifteen friends of Jane, all celebrating his return. Despite this being during the prohibition era, hard cider was available, but the group only consumed around five or six quarts. While Glatz and Zora were conversing in a corner of the camp, one Joseph Sussman, from a neighboring camp, approached Glatz and told him that he would kill a brother of Glatz the first time he saw him. Sussman continued to repeat this several times to Glatz, and Glatz finally resented this. Words were exchanged between the two, with fists following. As the fight developed, Matt Tomcic, from Sussman's camp, armed himself with a *go-devil* or large ax, used in splitting chemical wood and mixed himself up in the affair. Sussman, noticing that his friend was going to help him, also armed himself with a large shovel which was lying in the lobby of the camp.

As the fight continued raging for some time, Kordon, who did not take an active part in the battle, succeeded in getting himself out of the camp. While Kordon was outside of the camp, Tomcic appeared and proceeded to attack Kordon. Kordon, wanting nothing to do with the fight, fell trying to escape from the attack and received a terrible blow across his back from Tomcic. A few minutes later Kordon stood up and attempted to enter the camp, and just as he got to the door, Tomcic struck him on the back of the head with his *go-devil* and inflicted a wound that would eventually cause Kordon's death. Kordon, who had taken no part in the fight, unfortunately, received the worst injuries resulting from the fight. Immediately after the fight, Sussman and Tomcic left the scene and went back to their camp. Kordon's friends, Glantz and Zora, bandaged their friend's head and started for Saint Marys and eventually the Elk County Hospital in Ridgway. Kordon was admitted with two serious cuts to his head which caused considerable bleeding and evident damage to his skull. Both Glatz and Zora also suffered from cuts and bruising from the brawl but were able to return to their houses on Curry Avenue in Saint Marys after treatment.

Kordon lingered on at the hospital until the morning of Friday, March 11th, when he succumbed to his injuries and died. Death was listed as being caused by a fractured skull. Kordon's body was taken to the Meisel Undertaking Home in Saint Marys, where a Coroner's inquest was held on Saturday morning. The jury was composed of: A. G. Brehm, foreman, Dr. C. W. Boyer, D. J. Bagley, G. A. Mohr, Otto Zelt and J. A. Dippold. The jury heard from a number of witnesses, and the facts did not change from the original story told. What was also consistent in the testimony was that Kordon had at no time taken part in the fight. The jury deliberated for several minutes and then came back with the following verdict: "We find that James Kordon came to his death as a result of a blow inflicted on the skull with a piece of iron at the hands of Matt Tomcic. We find further that Joseph Sussman is an accomplice, in that he assisted in starting the fight in the course of which the fatal blow was struck."

Warrants were issued for the arrest of Matt Tomcic for murder and Joseph Sussman as an accomplice in the murder of Kordon. Officers traveled to Rathbun but could find no trace of either Tomcic or Sussman. Locals reported that the suspects had remained in Rathbun all week but had left in a hurry Saturday morning after hearing that Kordon had died of his injuries.

Ignac Kordon was born in Merna, Austria in 1883. He had come to Saint Marys a number of years earlier and had been employed at the tannery. He was described as a quiet and unassuming man and was never known to be quarrelsome but was of a peaceful disposition. He was well-liked and had many friends. He was survived by his wife, six small children living in Saint Marys, his parents and one brother and sister living in Austria and one sister living in Rathbun. His wake was held at his residence on Curry Avenue. The funeral took place at the Saint Marys Catholic Church with burial in the Saint Marys Catholic Cemetery.

Despite an exhaustive search for Tomcic and Sussman, they were never captured and never faced justice for this murder. Many years later, rumors developed that the suspects were living in West Virginia. This information was not followed up due to the expense of reopening the investigation and the amount of time it would have taken in those days to investigate this information.

Kordon's Tombstone in the
Saint Marys Catholic
Cemetery.

The Same Old Story

VENDERS OF MERCHANDISE.

As classified and appraised by the undersigned, duly appointed appraiser of Mercantile Taxes for the county of Elk, for the year 1865.

BREWERS IN THE BORO. OF ST. MARY'S.

Jos. Windfelder	9	25 00
C. H. Volk	9	25 00
Charles Haut	10	15 00
Michael Hantz	10	15 00

Article from *The Elk County Gazette* in 1865 announcing Charles Haut's Saloon Brewing License.

This case is the oldest chronicled murder that I could still find evidence of how the murder happened and the outcome. The earliest murder recorded in the Elk County Courthouse records was in 1845 when a Martha Wonder was charged with the murder of her husband. Martha was found not guilty. One of the hardest tasks in researching these old-time murders is finding the story and what came out at the trial. As very few newspapers were operating back in the mid-1800s, and even fewer copies survive, finding out what exactly happened is near if not impossible. I was lucky enough to find newspaper accounts and some trial material on this and the next murder. While these murders are not related, they do concern the same person, John Horack. And another similarity in these two cases was the consumption of alcohol, something which has caused murder and mayhem from the beginning of time up to and including the present day.

On June 24th, 1864, the Charles Haut Saloon in Saint Marys was the place to be. The saloon was featuring live music performed by a recent Hungarian immigrant, John Horack. Horack had learned to play the violin at the Royal Hungarian Academy of Music, in Budapest, in his earlier years. Horack came to America to follow his dream of playing for a professional band, but his dream had died when he took to alcohol in long days of unemployment, and when he did get a job, his alcoholism invariably caused him to fail. Horack had arrived in the relatively new settlement of Saint Marys in the early 1860s and had secured employment. On his days off, Horack played his violin in the local saloons and bars that would pay him in beer for his performance. Charles Haut had employed him on this particular Saturday afternoon, and Horack played his music from midday until late in the evening. Horack was served all the beer he could drink, and Horack took advantage of this deal, reportedly drinking more than his share. Haut announced the last call at eleven o'clock at night and told Horack he could go home and gave him two dollars, an amount they both had agreed upon earlier, in addition to all the beer he could drink. Horack, now extremely intoxicated, mumbled that his performance was worth more, but grudgingly accepted the money and left the saloon. Haut cleaned up the bar and retired upstairs to bed.

At around one o'clock in the morning, loud banging at the doors of the saloon awakened Haut and his boarder Joseph Krieg. Both of the men went downstairs and found several men, who asked Haut if he would open up and serve them some beer, as the other saloons in town had closed. They promised to make it worth Haut's time, and he relented. As more men entered the saloon and began to drink, Haut was indeed happy that he would be rewarded by these men, who were drinking heavily and purchasing whiskey shots to chase. All the men were loudly celebrating, when the saloon door opened and in walked John Horack, who had continued drinking after he had left the bar. Horack staggered up to the bar and ordered a beer. When Haut served him the beer and put his hand out for payment, Horack said he felt he was shortchanged earlier in the night and that the beer should be on the house. Haut called over Krieg and said that Horack said he was underpaid for the music he had performed earlier in the night. Krieg, who had made the initial arrangement for Horack to play that day, told Horack he was already well compensated for his music that day and in fact, he felt that with the large amount of beer Horack had consumed, he actually was overpaid. Horack then demanded six dollars for his performance, and Krieg responded by saying the performance was not worth six dollars and was not even worth six cents. Horack immediately struck Krieg with a closed fist, in which he had hidden a penknife. Krieg yelled that he was stabbed and staggered out of the barroom to seek safety. The other men at the bar jumped Horack and held him down until law enforcement arrived. Horack, who was a rather large man, attempted to fight them off, but in his intoxicated state, the men were easily able to hold him down onto the floor. Another patron went to arouse Dr. Blakely, who arrived shortly and attended to Krieg. Krieg was taken up to his bed on the second floor, and the doctor found that Krieg was stabbed in the right breast area. He dressed the wound and told Krieg he would return later in the day to check to see how he was progressing. The local police arrived and took Horack to the Saint Marys lockup, which then consisted of a single wooden jail cell.

Krieg lingered on until Tuesday, the 28th of June 1864, when he succumbed to his injuries. Krieg had developed an infection on Saturday evening, and this infection, resulting from the stab wound to his chest, was what eventually caused his death. In 1864, there were no antibiotics or treatment for infections and any breach of the skin could easily cause death. Doctors Blakely and Fessler performed a postmortem examination. The examination showed that the knife had entered the superior portion of the right breast, between the second and third rib, and also broke the second rib. An internal examination found that the right lung had collapsed with heavy internal hemorrhaging prevalent throughout the chest. Horack, who still was locked up in the Saint Marys Jail was now facing a murder charge.

Horack was transported to the Elk County Jail in Ridgway to await trial in the murder of Joseph Krieg. Horack was confined in the jail for over a year when his case was finally put before a grand jury in July of 1865. The Grand Jury returned a true bill against Horack, and the trial was scheduled to take place at the October session of the Elk County Court of Common Pleas in Ridgway.

The case of the Commonwealth versus John Horack commenced on Monday, October 2nd, 1865, at the Court House in Ridgway. President Judge R. G. White presided. District Attorney Blakely represented the Commonwealth, while Attorney's Souther and Hall represented the defendant. In pre-trial arguments, the defense was able to get the charge of first-degree murder *Nolle Prosequi*, or dismissed, with the remaining charges of manslaughter and assault proceeding in front of the jury. Charles Haut was the main witness for the prosecution. He testified as to what he had witnessed on the night of the assault. Doctors Blakely and Fessler testified as to the results of their post-mortem and the gentlemen who were in the saloon that night testified as to what they had observed. The defense offered that the stabbing was in self-defense, as Krieg had attacked Horack and he only drew the knife to protect himself when Krieg had thrown a punch and grabbed him by the neck. The Commonwealth and Defense then presented their final arguments to the jury which retired to render a verdict. The jury returned with a verdict of guilty to the charge of manslaughter. Judge White sentenced Horack to a term of six years imprisonment at the Western Penitentiary, and to pay a fine of one hundred dollars and the costs of prosecution. Horack was transported to the Western Penitentiary to serve out his sentence.

Joseph Krieg ended up buried in the Saint Marys Catholic Cemetery. His wooden grave marker disintegrated over the years and no longer exists. John Horack served out his six years in prison and returned to Saint Marys, none the wiser of his actions when drinking alcohol. He was soon to be involved in alcohol-related violence once again, and this time he was the loser in his fight. To be continued in the next story.

Karma

An old photo of the Zelt Hotel in Saint Marys, in front of which John Horack lost his life back in 1873. This building replaced the original Hotel in 1901. *Photo courtesy of Bill Auman.*

John Horack served his six-year prison sentence and was released in 1871. He returned to the streets of Saint Marys, a place he had grown to call home. The people of the town did not like the fact that a murderer was now living amongst them, and Horack was branded with the infamous "scarlet letter." Horack attempted to live a clean life after release and was a regular attendee at the Saint Marys Catholic Church for most of the first year he was free. Horack also avoided the taverns and saloons he was infamous for visiting and instead played his violin at church functions and outdoor concerts. Horack also began to work odd jobs around the Saint Marys area, and for some time he was beginning to build a reputation as a reformed man. All of that changed when he took a drink of alcohol in 1873 and went right back into living the rough life he had known prior. When he was intoxicated, Horack could not hold his temper, and he was banned from most of the drinking establishments in the town within a very short period. Horack, who had been a reliable hire when he was sober, also began to miss work engagements he had promised to do, and his reputation suffered. The scarlet letter that had begun to fade was now showing its bright red color.

Living in Saint Marys at this time was William Zelt. He had been a resident of the town since early childhood and had grown quite prominent and respected. Zelt owned the Zelt Hotel and Saloon which was located across from the post office in downtown Saint Marys. Zelt provided a dance hall for music, rooms to let upstairs and had a full bar which he had licensed to John Gerber. Zelt also held a personal grudge towards John Horack. The man that Horack had murdered back in 1864, Joseph Krieg, had been a personal friend of Zelt's. Zelt was known as a man who gave second chances. He had held back his animosity towards Horack and waited to see if the man truly was reformed as some had told him. He allowed Horack to perform at weekly music concerts he held at the hotel, under the condition that Horack does not imbibe on the premises while performing. This arrangement had worked out for some time, but when Horack went back to drinking, Zelt quickly banned him from performing anymore. After that, whenever Zelt would observe Horack in his establishment, he would swiftly let him know that he was not welcome there.

On Monday, June 2nd, 1873, the Zelt Hotel and Saloon was having live entertainment. Charles Luppes had been employed to play his clarinet in the music hall, which adjoined the bar room on the first floor. The bar was crowded all afternoon, with many local men enjoying the music. In the midst of this excitement,

John Horack had slipped into the bar unnoticed and had ordered a beer. The bartender, not realizing who this man was, served him several times. The proprietor, Zelt, who mingled with the customers, noticed Horack seated at the bar and went and spoke with Gerber. Gerber promised Zelt that he would evict Horack and went up to Horack and told him he had to leave as he was not welcome. Horack, who Gerber described as extremely intoxicated, complained that he was causing no trouble, and only wanted to speak with his fellow musician, Luppes. Gerber said he would get Luppes out of the music hall, so they could discuss what Horack described as serious business. Gerber summoned Luppes out of the music hall and Luppes and Horack discussed an upcoming music event they both would be playing. Horack then exited the barroom and immediately ran into Zelt, who was standing in front of the Hotel. Zelt immediately accosted Horack, telling him he was not welcome in his Hotel, and that if he showed up there again, Zelt would have him arrested. Horack, in an intoxicated state and known to have a temper, began to argue with Zelt. The loud argument had caused many in the bar to come to the door of the saloon to see what was happening. The men began to trade fists, and the commotion caused the dance and music to stop, as all now became interested in the loud ruckus taking place out on the sidewalk. Zelt had planted two prominent blows on the face of Horack, who fell off the wooden sidewalk and into the road. Zelt then picked up a rock from the road, and when Horack stood up, Zelt hit him in the back of the head causing Horack to stagger across the street and collapse. Zelt then went back into the bar. Patrons in the bar asked Zelt what had happened, and he replied; "I gave it to him…if Horack does not keep away from here, I'll give him more!"

Horack meanwhile lay in a heap on the road in front of the Hotel. Although it was already nine in the evening, a bright moonlit night made his body visible from some distance, especially due to the fact that he was dressed in a white shirt. The streets of Saint Mary were busy on this Monday evening, and many people witnessed the altercation between Zelt and Horack. Twelve-year-old Joseph Krug witnessed Horack falling and also heard what he said sounded like a board cracking when Horack fell. Young Krug, who was helping his father in his shop adjacent to the Zelt Hotel, went over to Horack and noticed he was not moving. Joseph ran into his father's shop and told him of what he had seen. Mr. John Krug went to the body of Horack and turned him over, so his face was upright. He splashed water in Horack's face and saw no movement. Several other gentlemen had gathered around Horack's body, and they picked him up and carried him onto the adjoining sidewalk. One of the bystanders, M. Barmettler, went for the doctor, while the other men washed Horack's face in an attempt to rouse him.

Justice of Peace G. C. Brandon arrived before the Doctor. He too attempted to arouse Horack with no success. Dr. Reynolds arrived shortly, and he examined the body and pronounced life extinct. Brandon directed that Horack's body be removed to the town hall building for an impromptu coroner's inquest. Dr. Reynolds was sworn in front of the jury and stated it would be necessary for him to conduct a post mortem examination before presenting his findings as to the cause of death. The inquest was adjourned until nine o'clock on Tuesday morning, while Dr. Reynolds carried out the autopsy. Justice Brandon meanwhile had ascertained that one Henry Schutzenback had been a witness to the fatal fracas and interviewed him. Schutzenback told Brandon that William Zelt had caused the fatal blows to Horack, and Brandon swiftly went to the Zelt Hotel and arrested Zelt on the charge of suspicion of murder, pending the outcome of the coroner's jury findings. Zelt was placed in the Saint Marys Jail.

At nine o'clock, Tuesday morning, the inquest was reconvened in the town hall. Doctors Reynolds and Hartman, who had already performed a post mortem examination over the body of Horack, testified that the deceased had received an injury on the back part of the head. This injury had caused congestion of the brain with strong effusion of blood on the brain, said wound being made by a blunt instrument, and was sufficient to cause death. Several other eyewitnesses to the altercation, including the Krug's and Schutzenback were then heard. The jury found the following verdict: "that said John Horack came to his death at the town of Saint Marys in the County of Elk on the evening of June 2nd, 1873, by being struck in the back of the head with a stone or other blunt instrument by William Zelt of Saint Marys, Elk County, Pennsylvania, making a gash or cut about two inches in length on the scalp and extending to the skull bone, and causing a mortal wound of which said Horack then and there died at the hour of half-past nine o'clock on the night of June 2nd, 1873." Zelt was ordered held in the jail, with a warrant now sworn out accusing him of murder in the death of John Horack.

William Zelt was taken before Elk County Associate Judge Wetmore on Tuesday evening, on a writ of habeas corpus and an application for bail was made by his attorneys McCauley and Bailey. J. K. P. Hall, Elk County District Attorney, did not oppose this motion and bail was set at $15,000. Zelt was able to put his Hotel up as collateral and was released on bail to await a forthcoming trial in the death of Horack. Sentiment in Saint Marys was almost totally in favor of Zelt, as he bore a solid reputation of being a quiet and industrious citizen. Horack, in contrast, was viewed as the direct opposite of Zelt. He was known as a man of intemperate habits, who often became mean and confrontational when he was under the influence of alcohol. The citizenry also knew that Horack had previously served a prison sentence for the death of a beloved resident, Joseph Krieg, and this would cause many to say he got what he deserved.

The trial of William Zelt took place in Ridgway on Monday morning, August 4th, 1873. Judge J. P Vincent was the presiding Judge, with Elk County District Attorney J. K. P. Hall representing the Commonwealth, and Attorneys McCauley and Bailey representing the defendant. The jury chosen included Wendlin Kunlin, Redford Segars, Peter Kemmerer, Abel Gresh, Charles Winslow, Philip Lesser, George Mohan, A. A. Clary, A. J. Rummer, J. W. Winslow, Charles Ritter, and Francis Frey. The courtroom was packed with citizens from Saint Marys, who had begun appearing on the early morning trains. The citizens of Saint Marys wholeheartedly supported Zelt, but many also came to observe how justice would be dealt with in such a situation. It was also noted that three murder trials were to take place during that week, Zelt, Donovan (included in this volume) and one for Mrs. Scott (which will be covered in a future edition). The Commonwealth called over fifteen witnesses who had personally observed Zelt strike Horack or who had observed the aftermath of the assault. The prosecution also called Doctors Reynolds and Hartman, who testified to their findings of the autopsy and who presented their opinion that the cause of Horack's death was directly related to the blow in the back of the head by Zelt, and the resulting stroke caused by the blow had caused Horack's death. The prosecution then rested.

The defense began by calling over twenty-five witnesses from Saint Marys, who testified to Zelt's good character and temperament. The defense then began calling witnesses who had known the deceased, and these witnesses testified to Horack's behavior when intoxicated and the many altercations that had resulted from his bad temperament. The defense also called Doctors Balfour and Hartley to the stand, and they gave their opinion that Horack had not necessarily died of a stroke brought on by the blow to the head, but had indeed expired due to his alcoholism, which caused his body to go into shock. The doctors for the defense did admit that it was possible that the blow to the head was the cause of death but left open their opinions that Horack's alcoholism was a contributory cause. The defense then rested.

The prosecution and defense presented their closing arguments on Wednesday afternoon, August 6th, 1873. The prosecution contended that Horack, no matter what his reputation or previous criminal record was, died as a result of the felonious assault by one William Zelt, who had directly caused his death and was therefore guilty of his murder. The defense countered that William Zelt was a model citizen, who had warned Horack many times to stay away from his Hotel, and when Horack challenged Zelt that night, they had got into a scrapple after Horack threatened Zelt. Zelt was defending his property and his life when he fought with Horack. The defense also brought up the possibility that although Zelt did indeed strike Horack in the back of the head with a rock, this was not definitively proven as the cause of death. Horack had more than likely died as a result of his extreme intoxication and not directly as a result of his injuries. The case then went to the jury.

The jury only retired for less than an hour when they returned. The jury pronounced a verdict of "guilty of manslaughter." Zelt's attorneys filed a motion for a new trial at once, and this was allowed by the Court. Zelt was admitted to bail in the amount of $2,000 and released. On Thursday, August 28th, 1873, Zelt appeared once again before Judge Vincent, having withdrawn his motion for a new trial and accepted the verdict of the jury. Judge Vincent sentenced Zelt to nine months incarceration in the Elk County Jail and a $400 fine.

Zelt served out his sentence in the Elk County Jail and returned to his wife and family in Saint Marys. He resumed proprietorship of his hotel and never had a run in with the law after this fateful incident. Zelt died at the age of fifty-four on January 22nd, 1899 and was buried in the Saint Marys Catholic Cemetery. The body of Horack was buried in an unknown location, more than likely a potter's field for the poor as he was described as being indigent. The whereabouts of his cherished violin was also never disclosed. It was also with some ironic fate that Horack had died within one hundred yards of where he had slain Joseph Krieg back in 1864. Karma is what some would call it.

James Lowers

Lowers House was located on the left, at the bottom of Grant Road.

James Lowers of Ridgway was a dedicated worker at the Eagle Valley Tannery in Ridgway. On Thursday, March 5th, 1931, he received news that he had some money coming to him from the bank and he could pick it up at any time. The money was the proceeds of a will from a distant relative that had finally been cleared. This was good news for Lowers, as he was living paycheck to paycheck and struggled like most people during the midst of the depression. Lowers informed his employer that he would be leaving work that day at noon and would be back to work the next day. Lowers also told his employer of his good fortune. Lowers left work at noon and stopped at the bank where he collected $60, which would be equivalent to over $900 in today's money. Lowers also stopped at the Grand Union Store on his way back to his residence on Grant Road. He purchased three loaves of bread and a package of tobacco. As Lowers strolled through town on his way to Grant Road, he stopped to talk with a friend, and eventually arrived at his shack where he planned to celebrate his good fortune.

On Friday, March 6th, Lowers failed to show up for work at the tannery. This was unusual, but with Lowers telling fellow workers about his windfall, they assumed he may have done too much celebrating the night before and had failed to wake up and make it to work. Saturday was an optional workday for employees, and even though Lowers did not show for work once again, his employers did not get aroused. On Monday morning, March 9th, when Lowers still did not show up for work, the alarm bells finally sounded for his employers. On that day, his employers also received a note from Lowers' neighbor, Mr. Dallenbach, who said he believed something was wrong with Lowers, as he had not seen his neighbor since Thursday night, and had been unsuccessful in contacting him since. Otto Glaus, the foreman at the Eagle Valley Tannery, took the note from Dallenbach and went and met with Chief Burgess C. L. Park. Mr. Glaus and Burgess Park then went to the Lowers residence to see if they could find out what was wrong with Lowers. When they arrived at the Grant Road residence, they found the back door open and found the body of Lowers lying on the floor in the front room of the home. They also observed a pool of blood about his head. They immediately contacted Elk County Detective Werner's office.

Detective Werner and Deputy Sheriff May arrived at the Lowers residence shortly after nine in the morning and secured the body of Lowers. Lowers had suffered a blow to the right side of his head which appeared to have crushed his skull. No other marks were found upon his body. Lowers was also clutching a package of tobacco. Werner observed that the residence was not ransacked, and it appeared that Lowers was struck from behind, as his body was lying on its stomach. An automobile tire was next to Lower's body. Werner believed Lowers was struck from behind by some blunt object while he was inspecting the automobile tire. Packages of bread were also laying on a table in the front room, unopened. Werner also noted that the pockets on Lower's pants were turned out and the belt he was wearing was slit. It was also noted that no money was found on the person of Lowers or in his residence. Elk County Coroner S. T. McCabe ordered the body removed to the Van Aken Funeral Home in Ridgway and deputized Dr. J. G. Flynn of Ridgway to perform an autopsy.

Dr. J. G. Flynn performed the autopsy on James Lowers. The autopsy revealed the following: three contusions, triangular position above right eye; upper lobe of right ear cut; cheek in front of ear cut and penetrates skull (fractures); compound comminuted fracture above the right ear, two inches square; scalp tissue crushed; lacerated wound of scalp at base of skull, penetrating skull; another lacerated wound at the back of the head. Lowers died of shock, hemorrhage of the brain and compression of the brain. The blows would have rendered him unconscious; however, the wounds would not have been immediately fatal, it was surmised that Lowers lived for several hours after the attack. Dr. Flynn stated that the implement that caused these injuries was more than likely a claw hammer. The position of the body, as it was found on the floor in the front room of his residence and the appearance of the room, indicated that the man was struck from behind and was never in a position to offer any resistance.

Detective Werner began the investigation by quizzing neighbors and friends of Lowers. One of the neighbors interviewed stated he saw a strange man in the front room of the house on Thursday afternoon. A fairly good description of this man was given, and Werner attempted to track him down.

Werner was certain that the man committing the act was friendly with Lowers and knew his habits and some of his business affairs. Werner also believed that the motive for this crime was money. He soon learned from some of Lowers friends, that Lowers had the habit of carrying large sums of money on his person and delighted in showing it to friends and even strangers. As Lower's pockets were rifled and his belt was sliced open, it was obvious that the perpetrator knew Lowers had money on him.

Werner next interviewed Thomas Lander, also from Grant Road. Lander said he had been with Lowers early Thursday afternoon and left him when Lowers went into the Grand Union Grocery Store on Main Street to purchase some tobacco and bread. Arthur Gifford, who resided near the Lowers residence, stated that he saw Lowers pass by with several loaves of bread in his arm about four-thirty, Thursday afternoon. As Werner found the loaves of bread unopened on a table in the Lowers residence, and also found Lowers clutching a tobacco package, he surmised that the murder must have taken place soon after Lowers returned home. Werner now began the hunt for the murderer.

James Lowers was around seventy years old in 1931. He was about six feet tall and weighed about one hundred and seventy-five pounds. He had lived in Ridgway for roughly fifteen years and had been steadily employed at the Eagle Valley Tannery. Lowers was single at the time of his murder. He had previously been married to a Mary Smith and had three children with her. When Mary died in 1900, Lowers married Margaret Mosher and had three more children with her. Lowers had been involved in a sordid crime some years earlier when he was sentenced to fifteen years in the Western State Penitentiary for assisting in the rape of his own thirteen-year-old daughter by a Frank Cornelli.

His wife Margaret also served fifteen years for the same incident. When Lowers and his wife were released from prison, Mrs. Lowers left her husband and took up with his brother, who was described as a vagrant. The new couple moved to Brookville. Lowers was still on state parole when the murder happened. When the Elk County Authorities called Lower's brother in Brookville after the murder, he expressed that he was sad to hear about the death, but he would pay no part of the burial expenses. It is interesting to note that the wake for Lowers was held at the Van Aken Funeral Home in Ridgway, and between eight hundred and one thousand people came to view the corpse. These large amounts of people were obviously drawn by morbid curiosity. When the funeral took place the following day, only one mourner was present, his neighbor Thomas Lander. Burial took place in Pine Grove Cemetery on Montmorenci.

Detective Werner had been working on two suspects he had identified through the interviews he had with Lowers' neighbors and friends. He had a warrant issued for the arrest of one Matt "Rhode Island Red" Cavanaugh, whose last known address was Mount Jewett. He was nicknamed "Rhode Island Red" due to his bright red hair. Corporal Eugene Stacey and Private Taylor of the Pennsylvania State Police Station in Kane and Clyde McKnall, former Police Chief of Kane and presently a deputy constable, were tasked with the arrest. On Wednesday evening, March 11th, the trio went to Mount Jewett, the last known residence of Cavanaugh, in search of their suspect. Despite an extensive search in Mount Jewett, they were unable to find Cavanaugh. The authorities then began to follow up on information they had received in Mount Jewett and were given an address in Kane as a probable location of where Cavanaugh could be found. On the following day, March 12th, the authorities surrounded the McDowell residence on Greeves Street in Kane. When they knocked on the door, Mrs.

McDowell answered the door. The officers inquired if Matt Cavanaugh was present at the house and Mrs. McDowell replied in the negative. The authorities insisted on searching the residence, and Mrs. McDowell relented. The officers found Cavanaugh and Mrs. McDowell's son Edward, hiding in a bed. Cavanaugh was immediately arrested and taken to Ridgway for interrogation. Werner had received information that Cavanaugh was the last person seen with Lower the day he was killed. According to reports at the time, Cavanaugh had been ordered previously to leave Kane, as he was arrested numerous times on public drunkenness charges. Cavanaugh had no known steady employment. He reportedly came from Ireland to America in 1921.

Cavanaugh had reportedly asserted earlier, that he had stayed at the Lowers home on Friday night and left early Saturday morning. As the medical examiner and Detective Werner believed Cavanaugh was killed on Thursday night, he was the main suspect. Cavanaugh also fit the description of the strange man that Lowers neighbor, Dallenbach, had seen at Lowers residence on Thursday evening. Detective Werner had the crime scene dusted for fingerprints and also had found a small baseball bat that was covered with blood and gray hair, and which now was considered the murder weapon. The bat was found hidden in Lowers house. Cavanaugh was held for five days and subjected to extreme interrogation by authorities. Cavanaugh repudiated a previous story in which he was quoted as admitting to police his presence in Lowers house on the day when physicians believe the man was clubbed to death. Cavanaugh maintained that he had visited Ridgway three weeks ago and was not present the week of March the 2nd, the week Lowers was killed. The State Police reconstructed his movements for the past week and a half and could not disprove his alibi that he was not in Ridgway at the time of the killing. Fingerprints found at the murder scene did not match Cavanaugh and with no physical evidence linking him to the murder, and no confession, the authorities had no option but to release Cavanaugh. On Tuesday, March 17th, Cavanaugh was released from custody with District Attorney Straub and Detective Werner admitting they had no evidence to hold him for the murder. Cavanaugh went back to Kane and once again took up residence in the McDowell home.

Detective Werner made a statement that a new arrest was imminent in the murder case and said he still had two suspects to question. On March 23rd, State Police at Kane arrested Edward McDowell, thirty-five of Kane and placed him in the Elk County Jail to await further investigation by the authorities. McDowell, during intense questioning, firmly stated that he had not been in Ridgway since February 22nd. Werner had previously been informed by witnesses, that McDowell had been seen in Ridgway on Thursday afternoon, March 5th, the alleged day of the murder. Werner brought in a fingerprint expert from the State Police Barracks in Butler to compare prints found at the murder scene on Grant Road with McDowell's. Several witnesses had testified that they saw McDowell walking down Race Street with Lowers on the day of the murder, and they once again were questioned. As McDowell was supposedly a close personal friend and frequent visitor to Lowers house, his fingerprints were expected to be found at the murder scene. Despite testing the "alleged" murder weapon for prints, none were found upon the weapon or person of Lowers that would implicate McDowell. McDowell was subject to an exhaustive interrogation for several days, but he did not give a confession to being involved in the murder. As Detective Werner only had circumstantial evidence, the testimony of witnesses that said McDowell was in Ridgway that fateful day, he was forced to release McDowell on the 25th of March.

No other suspects were ever developed in this case, and it entered into the unsolved murder file in Elk County. The presumption that the murder happened on Thursday, March 5th, after Lowers came back from town was borne out by the untouched loaves of bread on the table and the packet of tobacco clutched in his hands, items that were purchased by Lowers on his way home from work. The bank confirmed that Lower was given $60 that day, and this was never recovered, bolstering the robbery motive. The next-door neighbors, the Dallenbachs, also reported that they saw the strange man, resembling Cavanaugh, inside the residence shortly after four-thirty on the afternoon of March 5th and that they heard what sounded like a chair being knocked over around six-thirty that evening. They said the Lowers house was dark after that time and they never noticed the strange man leaving, but also never saw Lowers alive again. They said they went to his door and knocked every day until Monday, March 9th, and never received an answer. Cavanaugh and McDowell were described as close friends of Lowers and were frequent visitors to his house. The fact that the Dallenbachs did not specifically identify Cavanaugh or McDowell as the strange man seen at Lowers house was troubling. In reading the notes on the case, I believe the neighbors saw someone enter the Lowers residence and did not get a good of enough look at them to confirm their identity. Lowers brother was also a suspect in the case, as they were described as bitter enemies, and the brother was seen in Ridgway around the time of the murder. As the only "evidence" which Werner had was eyewitness testimony, which is often unreliable, that Cavanaugh and McDowell were seen in Ridgway on the day of the crime, and with no physical evidence linking them to the crime, the case was unsolvable. Modern forensic science certainly could have built a better case.

James Lower's Death Certificate

Rough on Rats

ROUGH ʘⁿ RATS TRADE MARK Unbeatable **RAT Exterminator** DONT DIE IN THE HOUSE

Why feed Rats? Rough on Rats kills 'em. Being all poison, one 15c. box will make or spread fifty or more little cakes that will kill fifty or more rats and mice. Though originally designed for Rats and Mice, experience has demonstrated it the most effective of all exterminators of ROACHES, ANTS AND BED BUGS, and it is the only thing at all effective against the large Black Cockroach or Beetle. 15c., 25c.

Fools the Rats, Mice and Bugs, but never disappoints or fools the buyer. Always does the work and does it right.

E. S. WELLS, Chemist, Jersey City, N. J., U. S. A.

John Latasin of Byrnedale was not having a good day on Tuesday, November 21st, 1905. He had woken up early in the morning with a stomach ache but had shrugged it off as he was expected to be at work in the coal mines later that morning. He had suffered an injury to his right arm recently and had been self-medicating the wound with salve he had bought at the local company store. The wound did not seem to be healing, but Latasin continued to apply the salve and new dressings daily. He also had recently begun to feel quite ill, often vomiting at his place of work. As medical assistance was quite expensive to the poor laborer, he did not seek out treatment, choosing instead to wait out the illness. Around noon time, the pain had enveloped all of the joints in his body, and he began to vomit uncontrollably. His coworkers helped him to his home, and he was placed in his bed, from where he would never leave alive again. Mrs. Latasin cared for her husband, who was in extreme agony. Latasin cried out in pain throughout the night, and by Wednesday morning his condition was critical. Mrs. Latasin sent for the local Doctor, Hays, who appeared shortly. Dr. Hays found Latasin in extreme pain and immediately suspected something was amiss. Mrs. Latasin told the Doctor that her husband was self-treating the wound on his arm with a "poison" he had bought at the local store. Dr. Hays discounted this salve as the cause of such pain and began to surmise that this was a case of poisoning, something he had seen in the past. Mr. Latasin was suffering from extreme body cramps and nausea, and his whole body was fraught with pain. Latasin lingered on with extreme pain for several days before finally succumbing early Friday morning. Nothing that Dr. Hays tried had alleviated the pain that Latasin was experiencing.

As Latasin lay dying, Dr. Hays alerted the local constable that he had a case of suspected poisoning. The constable was able to find, through investigation, that Mrs. Latasin had attempted to purchase "Rough on Rats" poison at the local store but was prevented from doing so by the store clerk. It was also learned that she then traveled to Tyler, where she was successful in her efforts to purchase the poison. Hays was also told that the Latasin's relationship was not a kosher one. A tenant in their house had taken a romantic interest in Mrs. Latasin, and she had reciprocated that affection. Mr. Latasin was aware of this scandal, and despite attempting to get the boarder to leave, he was unsuccessful in this endeavor. Mr. Latasin was so enraged by this affair that he went to his nearby sister's residence and transferred a life insurance policy from his wife's name to that of his sister. Latasin was also reportedly known to be afraid of his wife and often complained to his friends that she was evil.

Dr. Hays informed Elk County Coroner C. G. Wilson that his services were needed in Byrnedale on Friday evening, after the death of Latasin. Coroner Wilson traveled to Byrnedale on Saturday morning, November 25th and hastily convened an inquest. The principal witness was Dr. Hays, who provided his testimony of the illness and attempted treatment of Latasin, and how he suspected poisoning as the cause of death. The contents of Latasin's stomach were harvested and were sent to be analyzed. Testimony of Mrs. Latasin's purported affair and of her purchasing "Rough on Rats" was also presented. The evidence presented was deemed sufficient to arrest Mrs. Latasin for the murder of her husband, and she was taken to the Elk County Jail to await trial.

The trial of Annie Latasin for the poisoning murder of her husband took place on April 29th and 30th in the Elk County Court House in front of Judge McClure. District Attorney Baird represented the Commonwealth, while Dennis Driscoll represented the defendant. Doctor Hay's presented his testimony and the results of the analysis of the deceased's stomach. The contents of the stomach tested positive for a form of poisoning but whether it was from "Rough on Rats" or another form could not be discerned. Hay's did testify that poisoning via "Rough on Rats" could not be ruled out, however. Testimony was also elicited that Annie had indeed purchased the rat poison shortly before the death and that she was denied the poison at the Byrnedale store because of her "strange" behavior. The clerk in the store at Tyler testified that he did sell her the poison. Latasin's sister testified that he had told her about the rumored "affair" between his wife and his boarder. She also testified that this was well-known gossip in the tiny village. She testified about the changing of the life insurance policy and that Latasin had told her he was afraid of his wife. The Commonwealth then rested.

Attorney Driscoll began the defense by asserting to the jury that Latasin did indeed die from poisoning, but that the poison was not as a result of the "Rough on Rat's" that Annie had purchased, but the mysterious ointment that her husband was applying to the wound in his arm. Driscoll then called Annie Latasin to the stand to testify. Annie testified that she did purchase "Rough on Rats" in Tyler, but that it was necessary, as their residence had recently become invested with the vermin. She also said that after she had learned that the product was poisonous and that it would be fatal to her children if they ingested it, she threw it in the nearby stream. She testified that her husband was in fine physical condition until he had injured his arm in the mines. Her husband had acquired some type of ointment to treat the serious injury, and after he started applying it to his arm, he began to experience the pain and symptoms which would ultimately cause his death. Annie denied that she was having an affair and testified that one of the symptoms her husband was experiencing was paranoia.

The case was then referred to the jury for a verdict by Judge McClure who gave the jury a lengthy description of what reasonable doubt was. The jury then retired to contemplate their verdict. In less than an hour, the jury returned with a verdict of "not guilty." Judge McClure dismissed the jury and ordered Annie Latasin released from custody. What was a very compelling circumstantial case, was swayed by the lack of direct evidence that "Rough on Rats" was the cause of Mr. Latasin's demise. With the advance of forensics today, there more than likely would have been a different outcome. The jury did a good job in weighing the circumstantial "evidence" versus the reasonable doubt, and the win for Driscoll in this case helped to make his reputation as a competent defense attorney known. Mrs. Latasin returned to Byrnedale and her children after the verdict and was shunned by the local populace, who believed she had gotten away with murder. Her eventual whereabouts in the following years is not known. Mr. Latasin was buried in Saint Joseph's Cemetery in Force, in an unmarked grave.

Dennis Driscoll, esquire, the defense attorney for Mrs. Latasin.

A Little Pepper for Your Booze

Joseph Dudack's Death Certificate

In the case that follows this story, I will be writing about the "murder" of Mrs. Tozier by one Mary Dudack. In researching that case, I found death had visited the Dudack residence at Indian Run not once, but twice, within a short period of time. The mysteriousness of this case, as well as the location of the death, makes it a perfect addition and preview to the next chapter.

Joseph Dudack was thirty-six years old in 1907. He had emigrated from Poland, then a part of the Imperial Russian Empire, around the turn of the century and had ended up in Elk

County, where he secured employment as a laborer in the lumber industry, then prevalent in the Village of Glen Hazel. Joseph had married Mary Dudack, and they had five children. Dudack had moved his family into a two-room shack that was located at the head end of Indian Run, on the Bendigo Road. In reading the newspaper accounts of arrests during their married life, it became evident that the Dudack marriage was one of domestic violence, perpetrated by both husband and wife. Joseph had a reputation as an alcoholic, who became mean and belligerent when he was drunk, while Mary bore a reputation as a "loose" woman, who was accused of running a "bawdy" house on several occasions. Mrs. Dudack was also known to drink heavily, and physical fights often took place between the married couple when both of them were drinking. One of the recorded fights was in *The Johnsonburg Press* of November 6th, 1903, when Mary, accompanied by her five children entered Johnsonburg to seek medical attention for a bad scalp wound, inflicted by her husband during a fight. Mary stated her husband had hit her over the head with a plate and had made the family vacate the residence on this cold day, while under the influence of alcohol. When the authorities went to the Dudack residence to question Joseph, he was found to have absconded from the area, and he did not appear back for some time. He was not charged over the incident, as Mary declined to press charges.

The Dudacks lived this life of alcohol and debauchery for the next four years, getting into regular physical fights with each suffering wounds to some extent or another. The relationship could be described as a love-hate one, with neither caring how their children viewed their extreme behaviors. Mary Dudack earned her living as a prostitute during these years and often entertained local men from the surrounding area. Mrs. Dudack also enjoyed her alcohol, and never missed a chance to imbibe, whether she had parental duties to look after or not. Rumors also arose that Mary was also growing tired of her husband and was discussing divorcing him or finding some other way to drive him out of their home. When Mary was drunk, she also told confidants that she wished Joseph would die and said she would not miss him and his violent ways.

On Friday, November 2nd, 1907, Joseph arose early and told his wife he was going hunting. He was feeling unwell for the last several months and had, what he described, as the flu that would not leave. He also complained of weakness in his joints and struggled to keep up with the physical demands of being a lumberman. What his illness did not affect was his thirst for alcohol. He imbibed at every possible occasion, and he decided this day would be no different. As Mr. Dudack was walking along the road heading towards Glen Hazel, he met Steve Zimmerman and James Misko, two gentlemen from the nearby settlement of Rasselas, and drinking companions of his. As the trio spoke, Dudack heard that they were headed to Johnsonburg to purchase provisions and Dudack asked them to bring several bottles of alcohol back to his cabin for an afternoon drinking bout. Dudack also mentioned to the Rasselas duo, that he was feeling quite unwell as of late, but that the effects of alcohol always made his pain go away. Zimmerman and Misko continued their travels to Johnsonburg, while Dudack returned to hunting along the roadside.

Zimmerman and Misko appeared at the Dudack residence early in the evening and brought with them a bottle of brandy and a bottle of grain alcohol. Both of the men had spent the day drinking heavily in Johnsonburg and wanted to keep the party going when they arrived. Mary joined Dudack, Zimmerman, and Misko, and the brandy was the first drink of choice. A quantity of pepper was added to the brandy, as was common in those days, to make the drink hotter. The party continued in boisterous fashion, with Mary entertaining the young Misko while Zimmerman and Joseph spoke of the lumber industry and how the lack of new timber cuttings was causing jobs to be scarce. Soon the brandy was gone, and Zimmerman went to this wagon outside to fetch the bottle of grain alcohol. The oldest son of the Dudacks accompanied him out to the wagon. Zimmerman secured the bottle of grain and added some "pepper" to the bottle, which he had in his pocket. They then returned to the cabin. Dudack poured himself a generous glass of the grain, and when he took a drink, he immediately became violently ill. Zimmerman helped Dudack to his bed. Dudack began to vomit, and he developed a fever. Zimmerman and Misko left the residence to head to Rasselas around seven o'clock as Dudack was no longer able to party.

Dudack remained in his bed and vomited the entire night and into the next morning. Mr. Dudack lingered on until around six in the morning, when he expired. Mrs. Dudack hastily went to Johnsonburg to inform the authorities. Squire Secrist and Constable McClintic headed towards Indian run and the home of Dudack, upon hearing of his death. While examining the body of Dudack, his eldest son stated that he followed Zimmerman out to his wagon, when he retrieved the bottle of grain. Young Dudack also stated that he saw Zimmerman empty contents of a paper he had in his pocket into the bottle before returning to the house. He then said he watched his father drink some and then his father fell ill. Constable McClintic had the body of Dudack removed to the funeral parlor of Ubel & Flynn to await an autopsy to be conducted by Dr. Sharp. Dr. Sharp was informed of the allegations by young Johnnie Dudack, and when he was unable to find a physical cause of death for Dudack, he removed Dudack's internal organs.

Dr. Sharp appointed a coroner's jury on Monday morning in Johnsonburg. Members of the jury included Alva Gregory, George Younger Sr., J. Weis, and W. Tuttle. The jury heard the testimony of both Zimmerman and Misko who recounted meeting Dudack on the way to Johnsonburg and how they stopped at the residence on the way back, after a long day of drinking and shared their alcohol with the Dudacks. They also repeated how they added pepper to both of the bottles of alcohol for the hotness it provided. The jury then heard from Mrs. Dudack, her son John and her daughter Mary. They all told relatively the same story. Zimmerman held to the story that he added pepper to both of the bottles, and when questioned about what young John had said, he stated it was pepper and nothing else. Dr. Sharp then presented that he could find no natural reason for the death, and then presented the internal organs and the bottle of grain in question and stated he would send these to the chemist to be analyzed for any poison they may contain. He would recall the jury when the results were delivered, and the jury could make a determination at that time. Dr. Sharp then marked the cause of death on the certificate as unknown. The jury was then adjourned until further "evidence" was obtained.

The body of Joseph Dudack was placed in charge of the Elk County Commissioners, as Mrs. Dudack claimed penury. The Commissioners had the remains interred in the Elk County Home for the Poor Cemetery in Saint Marys. The chemist's report arrived several weeks later, with a finding that no poison was discovered in either the bottle or the internal organs. Dr. Sharp reconvened the jury, and the death was determined to have been from unknown causes. In less than two months, tragedy would once again visit the Dudack residence, with Mrs. Dudack as the central character.

Debauchery

The entrance to Indian Run on the Johnsonburg-Bendigo Road. The Dudack house was located at the head end of this stream.

On the night of January 18th, 1908, Angelo Coppolo of Indian Run, located near Johnsonburg, was awakened by loud screaming at his front door. Angelo recognized the voice as coming from his neighbor, Mrs. Joe Dudack, who lived in a shack of known debauchery which was located at the head end of Indian Run. Mrs. Dudack was asking for Coppolo to open the door and let her in, but Coppolo, knowing the reputation of his neighbor, refused to and told her to go away. After several attempts to open his door, Mrs. Dudack left, and Coppolo went back to bed without the slightest care about what his neighbor had come to tell him. Dudack then went to Johnsonburg and was seen by several persons with blood on her face and hands, which she variously described as coming from a nosebleed earlier while being in bed, and later she said the blood came from breaking out a window when her house burned down. Dudack mentioned a mysterious man had been at her home the previous night, but somehow failed to mention that anyone had died in the flames.

Coppolo woke up on Monday morning and wondered why Mrs. Dudack had been to his door the previous night. He decided to visit her residence at the head end of Indian Run. When he left his house, he noticed his doorknob was covered in blood and surmised that the blood had come from Mrs. Dudack the previous night, as she had grasped his door handle to try to gain admittance. He then walked up Indian Run to the Dudack residence. He found the entire house had been consumed by fire. He looked around in the ashes and noticed a human skeleton. Coppolo hastened to Johnsonburg to report his grisly find, which he first thought might have been his neighbor, Mrs. Dudack.

The Dudack home was a known "bawdy" house or house of prostitution. Many criminal investigations and arrests had taken place there over the years due to illegal liquor sales, prostitution and various incidents of public indecency. The people of Johnsonburg were well aware of Mrs. Dudack and the goings on in her house. Only two months previous, an investigation had taken place there over the untimely death of her husband, Joe Dudack, a case discussed previously in this book. The reputation of Mrs. Dudack and the house she kept explains why her "neighbor" Coppolo, was reluctant to open the door to her late on Sunday night.

Coppolo went into Johnsonburg and stopped at the police station to report what he had found. Police Chief McLaughlin and Constable McClintic listened to Coppolo's story about Mary Dudack visiting his residence the previous night and that he found blood on the door handle in the morning before he visited the Dudack house and found it incinerated. Chief McLaughlin had already been made aware of Mrs. Dudack appearing in town earlier in the morning, with blood on her face and her clothes. Mrs. Dudack had told a story of breaking a window to get out of her house due to the fire, and that is how she cut herself. She had told authorities at that time that no one else was in the house, as the "man" had already left. Mrs. Dudack had holed up in the Johnsonburg Hotel, and the authorities were not going to investigate the matter further until Coppolo arrived. With Coppolo's story of a skeleton in the ashes of the house, Chief McLaughlin proceeded immediately to the Hotel to interview Mrs. Dudack again and to have her accompany the authorities to her now burned house.

Mrs. Dudack was questioned on the way to her residence by the police, and she now changed her story once again. She said she and a Mrs. Tozier had gotten into a fight at her house late last night, over a young man that had been living in her house. Mrs. Tozier did not want this young man to leave, and Mrs. Dudack refused to let him stay any longer. The argument erupted into a physical altercation, and Mrs. Dudack claimed that Tozier armed herself with a razor and lunged at her; Dudack claimed to have fought off Tozier and sustained injuries to her face during the fight. This, despite no wounds being found on Dudack's face or hands to explain the blood. She also claimed that Tozier had set fire to the house while she was inside, and she had escaped and went to her neighbor's the Coppolo's for assistance. She would also not divulge the name of the "young man" which the fight supposedly started over, only saying he left prior to the incident. When the party arrived at the house, they found the two-room building totally burnt to the ground. Coppolo showed the Police Chief where he found the skeleton and clearly visible in the ashes was the skeleton of a human being, burnt almost to ashes. Dudack retold her story once again while surveying the ruins of her home and when she stepped into the ashes, she kicked the skull, and it almost totally disintegrated into powder. She exclaimed loudly that this was the post from her bed and not a skeleton. The police quickly removed her from the scene and began to collect the bones. The police also collected a razor and an ax close to the remains. Dudack was taken to the Elk County Jail at this time, and the Elk County Coroner was called.

Elk County Coroner E. B. Sharp appointed a jury composed of P. J. Heslin, Jacob Bassinger, Joe Haley, George Younger, M. W. Murphy, and B. M. Bush. The first witness heard was Angelo Coppolo and his son John who lived near the Dudack home. Mrs. Dudack came to their door at about eleven o'clock on Sunday night, the 19th of January, and aroused the family. She said her house was burning, but Coppolo felt he could do nothing to put out the fire and decided not to let her in his house. He stated he visited the ruins the next morning and saw the skeleton in the ashes. He said he did not disturb them but immediately notified the police in Johnsonburg of what he had found. Next to testify was Tom Lewis, who stated he had been at the Dudack home on Saturday afternoon and saw the Tozier woman there. John Moran and Mrs. Walter Scott testified as to what Mrs. Dudack told them when she came to town at an early hour on the 19th of January. Mrs. Dudack was then called to testify, but her story was such that the jury could not understand the ramblings which incriminated herself, as she admitted that she had fought with Tozier over a young man and that Tozier burnt the house during the melee. The District Attorney presented that Mrs. Mary Tozier fought for her life with a razor as her only weapon, against a heavy woodsman's ax in the hands of her jealous friend and companion, only to be struck down and left to die, while the house was burned over her head to conceal the crime. The ax and razor found next to the charred skeleton were presented to the jury as the evidence of a fight, and Chief McLaughlin presented his testimony that Dudack had kicked the skull of the deceased when she had been at the ruins. McLaughlin said when he challenged Dudack that she had kicked the skull; Dudack said it was not a skull, but only her old bedpost. Evidence was also presented that Dudack's face and hands were covered with blood when she came to town to report the fire, but no wounds were found upon her body. In view of the facts presented to the jury, they returned a verdict that in their opinion, Mrs. Tozier came to her death at the hands of Mrs. Dudack, who afterward set fire to the house to hide the crime and recommended that she be held to await the action of the grand jury at the next term of court. Dudack was then taken to jail at Ridgway.

The trial of Mary Dudack began at the Elk County Courthouse on April 17th, 1908. District Attorney Baird represented the Commonwealth while Attorney Flynn represented the defendant. Judge Harry Alvin Hall presided. The selection of the jury took an inordinate amount of time because the Commonwealth was pushing capital punishment, while the evidence presented was all circumstantial. When the jury pool was questioned whether they could decide a case based on circumstantial evidence, many were unfavorable to convicting of capital punishment on such evidence. The last prospective juror from the pool was chosen as the twelfth juror, thereby avoiding the calling of additional prospective jurors. In the days of the trial, women were never called on capital cases as they were thought to be too delicate to hear such evidence that would be presented. The jury was composed of: Frank Geeck, Barber, Saint Marys, Gus Harps, Laborer, Ridgway Township, Rex Gray, blacksmith, Jay Township, J. W. Gorman, J. Bouler, Ridgway, Hector McDonald, liveryman, Ridgway, Anton Gahn, laborer, Benezette, Jeremiah Beck, farmer, Fox Township, W. H. Deveraux, Wilcox, W. C. Winslow, clerk, Shawmut; C. E. Kline, painter, Ridgway and William Weidert, farmer, Wilcox.

Angelo Coppolo was the first witness called to the stand. He stated that Mrs. Dudack had come to his house at about eleven o'clock on the night of January 18th and wanted to come into his house. He refused to let her in, and she left after a little while. Coppolo stated that he found blood on the doorknob the next morning when he went outside and stated that Dudack had been trying to open his door the previous night by turning the locked doorknob. Coppolo stated he then went to the Dudack house, found it incinerated, observed the skeleton and went to Johnsonburg to report his findings. He stated he did not disturb the scene at any time. Chief of Police McLaughlin, Constable McClintic, John Moran, Siegfried Byburg and Mrs. Walter Scott all testified as to Mrs. Dudack's actions on the night in question, when she came to Johnsonburg, and on the following day. Almost every story she told to each of these individuals was materially different and involved conflicting circumstances. Dudack told some that the blood on her face and hands came from breaking glass to escape the flames, that she had a bloody nose that night and that she had fallen and cut herself after leaving the house and this is where the blood came from. An examination of her body at the time of her arrest revealed no cuts which would have caused the blood. Chief of Police McLaughlin testified that Mrs. Dudack told him there was a man at her home but did not mention anything about the Tozier woman. He asked her where Mrs. Tozier was, and she said, "Poor Mary's gone, she was burned in the house." She said she and Mary had quarreled over the man. To Mrs. Scott she told a story of a quarrel with Mrs. Tozier, the latter threatening her with an ax, and as an excuse for the blood that was on her clothing when she first came to town, she said that two men came to her home and beat and choked her. Then she and Mrs. Tozier went to sleep, and during the night she was aroused by the flames which destroyed the house, and that the blood on her face and blouse came from when she broke out a window to escape the flames. Constable McClintic testified that Dudack had told him that Mrs. Tozier drove her out of the house with a revolver. She later told McClintic that an ax was used for that purpose and not a revolver. She admitted that a fight had taken place between her and Mrs. Tozier. The trial then recessed for the day.

The trial resumed on Friday morning with Constable McClintic testifying about finding the skeleton in the ruins of the house, in company with Chief of Police McLaughlin. The bones were then presented as evidence and according to court reporters; they looked very much like a scrap pile of burned bones. The only part that could have been recognized by laymen was a portion of the skull. McClintic, McLaughlin and Angelo Coppolo then testified that the bones, when first found in the ruins, presented the shape of a human skeleton, but that they had been broken somewhat in getting them out of the ashes. McClintic then testified that an ax and a razor were found near the body and that Mrs. Dudack had told him that she always kept an ax and a razor in the house. Thomas Lewis then testified that he had seen the Tozier woman at the Dudack house on the afternoon of January 18th, and he had not seen her since. David Street, of Glen Hazel, said that Mrs. Tozier lived with Joe Long near Glen Hazel for the past five or six years. He had seen her frequently during that time but had not seen her since last December. William Riley and Fred Fitch, also from the same neighborhood, testified to the same thing. The Commonwealth then rested.

Juror C. E. Kline had meanwhile taken ill during Thursday night, but when court convened Friday morning, he stated that he thought he could hold out until the conclusion of the case. However, during the morning, he was again taken violently ill, and after consultation with the attorneys, it was decided to accept his absence from the jury, and he was accordingly discharged. It was then made a part of the record to continue the case with eleven jurors, the defendant waiving exceptions and any advantage that might occur from the discharge of the juror.

Attorney Flynn then began the defense by raising the question that "corpus delicti" had not been proven. Flynn argued that the Commonwealth must show that a crime had been committed and that a certain person had been killed, and this crime must be established independently and outside of admittance or confession by the defendant. The defense contended that the corpus delicti had not been established, that it had not been proven that Mary Tozier was dead. The prosecution stated it was shown Mary Tozier had been in the house on the afternoon preceding the night of the fire, that there were human remains found after the fire, and that the defendant had left the house at the time of the fire. The prosecution said that the defendant had blood spots on various parts of the person, all of which was evidence outside of any admission made by the defendant. Flynn then asked the Judge to instruct the jury on the point of corpus delicti. Attorney Flynn said he was willing to submit the case to the jury on the evidence produced by the Commonwealth and he did not call any witnesses for the defense. He summed up the case to the jury by stating that as no positive identification had been made of the burnt pile of bones presented, no evidence of a murder was presented, and no admission of guilt by his charge was admitted, no crime had been shown to have been committed, and his client should be acquitted as there was nothing to answer for.

District Attorney Baird then presented his summation to the jury by stating that circumstantial evidence pointed to the fact that Mary Tozier was the skeleton found in the ashes of the Dudack house, that Mrs. Dudack was covered with blood despite having no cuts or abrasions to justify the blood. The testimony of acquaintances of Mary Tozier that she has not been seen since the fire is also evidence that Tozier was the victim of the fire. The Commonwealth presented that a drunken fight had taken place between the women over a young man whom Mrs. Dudack did not want to reside in the house and whom Mrs. Tozier did. The verbal argument ended up in a physical fight in which Dudack armed herself with a large ax, and Tozier was no match. Baird said the blood on Dudack was the result of blood splattering on her when she hit and eventually murdered Tozier. Dudack then set the house on fire to hide her crime. The Commonwealth then rested.

Judge Hall then gave an exhaustive charge to the jury, defining corpus delicti. Standards back in that time were not as defined as they are today. From Wikipedia: "*Corpus delicti* is one of the most important concepts in a murder investigation. When a person disappears and cannot be contacted, many police agencies initiate a missing person case. If during the course of the investigation, detectives believe that he/she has been murdered, then a "body" of evidentiary items, including physical, demonstrative and testimonial evidence, must be obtained to establish that the missing individual has indeed been murdered before a suspect can be charged with homicide. The best and easiest evidence establishment in these cases is the physical body of the deceased. However, if a physical body is not present or has not yet been discovered, it is possible to prove a crime took place if sufficient circumstantial evidence is presented to prove the matter beyond a reasonable doubt. For example, the presence at a missing person's home of spilled human blood, identifiable as that person's, in sufficient quantity to indicate exsanguination., demonstrates—even in the absence of a corpse—that the possibility that no crime has occurred, and the missing person is merely missing, is not reasonably credible." The jury then deliberated for several hours and returned with a verdict of "not guilty."

The lack of investigative tools in 1910 doomed this case. In reading the reports of this case and the circumstantial evidence that was collected, I believe it was Mary Tozier whose remains were found in the burned-out shack of Mrs. Dudack. It is interesting to note that although the Pennsylvania State kept and recorded all death certificates from 1906 until the present day, I could find no such record of a death certificate for Mary Tozier. It is apparent that because of the condition of the burnt skeleton, no autopsy was conducted, and because no positive identification of the skeleton was possible, the Commonwealth was not able to prove Tozier was deceased. Today this case would have provided a much different conclusion. The bones of "Mary Tozier" were buried in the Elk County Home grounds in Saint Marys. I could not find what happened to Mary Dudack after the trial. I do believe however she moved to eastern Pennsylvania and died there many years later.

Joseph Zampogna

Zampogna was murdered under the streetlight on the right, on
Blaine Avenue.

On the 4th of July 1933, Joseph Zampogna of Johnsonburg
was out celebrating. Not only was Zampogna celebrating the
Nation's birthday, but he was also celebrating the completion

and opening of the Grant Street Bridge, a bridge his construction company had won the state contract for to construct, and which opened for public travel on July the 3rd. Zampogna visited his friend, Mike Torchia, for several hours and then went to the Palm Inn Restaurant on Market Street. Zampogna then left the restaurant and headed towards his home at around ten thirty at night. The Fourth of July fireworks display was in progress, and the residents were out celebrating the Nation's independence. Zampogna must have been proud as he drove across the great new Grant Street Bridge on the way to his home located at 216 Blaine Avenue. (It is interesting to note that 216 Blaine Avenue was also the residence of Dominic Scopiletti, the infamous pickle barrel murder, who was murdered previously in Johnsonburg in 1926.)

As Zampogna entered Blaine Avenue, he observed several children blocking the road on the way to his house. He stopped his car at the slight corner on Blaine Avenue to allow the children to disperse. He was four houses away from his residence. The children also left a traffic horse in the middle of the road and Zampogna parked his auto to remove this barrier. As he stepped out of his automobile, a figure emerged from the shadows and pointed a gun at Zampogna. In a flurry of bullets, Zampogna fell, death being instantaneous from a bullet wound to the head. The figure then walked up and pumped a total of nine bullets into the prone body of Zampogna and casually strolled away into the shadows.

As this was the 4th of July, and as the public fireworks display was in progress, the streets of Johnsonburg, including Blaine Avenue, were full of spectators watching the show. Numerous people were lighting off their personal fireworks, and the noise masked the shots which took Zampogna's life.

Peter Gasbarre was driving home to his residence on Blaine Avenue when he came upon the crumpled body of Zampogna lying in the middle of the street. He stopped his truck and went out to check on Zampogna. He saw that Zampogna was dead. As Gasbarre stood over the body, he observed Eugene Jacob walking down the street. Gasbarre, who did not know the victim, called Jacob over to the body. Jacob, who lived in close proximity to Zampogna, immediately identified the body as his neighbor. As the men were talking over the body, Joe Galdini came along in his car and also stopped. Jacob told him about the murder and asked him for a ride into town to notify the authorities. Galdini drove Jacob to the Johnsonburg Police Station where Night Patrolman Ives was on duty. Jacob notified Ives of what he found, and Ives immediately set out for Blaine Avenue.

Ives notified Elk County Detective Leo Werner, Constable Buzzard, Chief of Police McMurray and a member of the State Constabulary who all hurried to Blaine Avenue. The murder scene was secured, and the authorities began to canvass the area to see if anyone could offer any clues to this gruesome slaying. Besides Gasbarre, who left immediately after giving his statement, the only other "witnesses" they found were two young girls who said they walked by the scene of the shooting at around ten thirty for a short walk to the new Grant Street Bridge. When they walked back a mere five minutes later, they saw the body of Zampogna lying in the street. They said they saw no one, heard nothing and said that no vehicles passed them as they strolled. Zampogna's body was removed to the Ubel Undertaking Rooms to await an autopsy and subsequent coroner's jury. Elk County Coroner, Dr. S. T. McCabe was notified of the shooting. McCabe was attending the celebrations in Kane at the time and immediately set out for Johnsonburg upon hearing of the killing. Zampogna's auto, with the headlights on and the engine running, was inspected to see if there was any sign of a struggle in the driver's compartment. The vehicle, without the parking brake on and in neutral, was found to be void of any signs of violence. Zampogna's wife and brothers returned home from the Kane celebration while the scene was being investigated and were mortified to discover the victim was their loved one.

Joseph Zampogna was thirty-eight years old in 1933. He was born in Italy and had immigrated to the United States in 1905. He lived in Johnsonburg since 1913. He was married to Perranna Zampogna and resided at 216 Blaine Avenue. Zampogna's three younger brothers, Reynold, Adolph, and Ralph also resided with him. He also had a sister in Italy. Zampogna had served in the United States Army during World War One in France. He returned to Johnsonburg after the war and went into the construction business. Zampogna was fortunate enough to secure sub-jobs for excavating, sewer and drainage trenches on the Pennsylvania State Roads. He was the contractor who cleared the site for the Ridgway Waterworks Reservoir and was the contractor and foreman on many of the "Pinchot" road jobs, a depression era program named after Governor Pinchot, done in Elk County in the two years before his death. He was awarded the contract for the construction of the new bridge over the Clarion River on Grant Street and hired local union workers as well as W. E. Clark as his foreman. His younger brothers also worked with him in his construction endeavors. The Grant Street Bridge was his last job as a contractor and opened to travel only the day before his slaying.

An autopsy was performed by Coroner McCabe at the Ubel Undertaking Parlors. McCabe found that death would have been instantaneous. He found a total of nine bullets had entered Zampogna. One bullet entered the left side of the neck and lodged in the right arm. One bullet entered the right ear and lodged in the left side of the brain. One bullet entered the left side of the face under the eye, in which the bullet took a downward course, knocked out one tooth and spread the other teeth in the jaw upward. One bullet entered the front of the chest around the second rib, went through the spine and lodged under the skin of the back. One bullet entered the left side of the abdomen. One bullet entered the left thigh and followed up the thigh bone on an upward course and lodged in the muscles close to the spine. One bullet entered the front of the left ear, took an upward course and came out of the skull above the right ear. One bullet glanced through the right side of the chest above the shoulder, and one bullet went through the right forearm, breaking the bone. McCabe was able to extract four slugs from the body, the other five having passed through the body. He was able to determine that the weapon used was a .32 caliber weapon.

McCabe convened an inquest on July the 10th at his offices in Johnsonburg. The jury was composed of Alva Gregory as foreman, John Grumley, George Cherry, Leo Maloney, James Beyer, and Emil Petzold. Ms. Marjory Marvin was the stenographer. Only three witnesses were heard. Peter Gasbarre, a truck driver, testified that he was the one who first saw the body in the street. He was driving to his home on Blaine Avenue and was forced to stop when he saw the body of Zampogna lying in the street. At the same time, he saw Eugene Jacob walking along the street. Together they approached the body. Gasbarre testified he did not identify the body and did not know who the deceased was until the next morning. On his way to Grant Street, he said he met no foot traffic and saw no cars or trucks. He also stated that all houses in the vicinity of the murder seemed dark. He remained at the scene for about five minutes after Night Policeman Ives came, and then he went home. He said he mentioned the incident only to his wife that night. He said it was approximately twenty minutes from when he saw the body until Jacob and Galdini returned with the police.

Eugene Jacob testified similarly but said he identified the dead man at once as he had known Zampogna for three months. Jacob also knew Zampogna's car well, often seeing it parked in front of his house. Galdini, who came along in his car and accompanied Jacob to the police station testified as to the scene as the other two did. All three said they saw no one around the vicinity, heard no unusual noises, did not notice any cars along the street except Zampogna's Ford and Gasbarre's truck.

McCabe then testified as to the nine separate bullet wounds he uncovered at the autopsy. No other information or witnesses were heard from, and the case was given to the jury. The jury then returned the verdict that "Deceased came to his death on the night of July 4th, 1933, from multiple gunshot wounds at the hand or hands of persons unknown to the jury."

The funeral for Joseph Zampogna was held on Saturday, July the 8th, from the Holy Rosary Church in Johnsonburg. The Reverend A. H. Wiersbinski officiated and delivered an impressive funeral address. Pallbearers were Joseph Marrone, Ellis Vedanta, Patsy Casilio, Dominic DiNardo, Jack Cannella, and James Dinlio. Out of town relatives and guests attended from Pittsburgh, Buffalo, Kane, Westline, Saint Marys, Mount Jewett, and Ridgway. Over fifty cars and massive floral arrangements accompanied Zampogna to his final resting place in the Wardvale Cemetery. Law enforcement, undercover in plain clothes, mingled with the mourners in an unsuccessful attempt to identify if the perpetrator(s) were present.

Elk County Detective Leo Werner issued a statement to the press that they were actively seeking the last person that Zampogna was observed speaking to when he was leaving the Torchia home on Center street. It was known that Zampogna had left Center Street and parked on Market Street, where he was observed by several people speaking to an unknown man. This was at around ten-thirty on the night of the murder. The authorities also discounted that this was a "hit" by organized crime. The brutal nature of the killing and the overkill in the number of bullets pointed this to be as a result of a personal grudge, one that authorities believed had occurred within three months of the slaying. Werner found that the Italian Community in Johnsonburg was close-lipped on any information related to the slaying. Werner also observed that the shades were pulled on all of the houses on Blaine Avenue and the residents would not answer their doors when the authorities came knocking. He appealed to any "Americans" in possession of any information to contact him immediately, and all information would be held in strict confidentiality. Werner traced the movements of Zampogna on the day before the slaying and went to Byrnedale and Ridgway retracing his steps. He publicly exclaimed that the murder was an act of extreme revenge. He also lamented the fact that the murder took place directly under a bright street light, with many people purportedly watching the firework display on Blaine Avenue, yet no one was willing to come forward with any information. This silence was understandable, due to the perceived involvement of the Black Hand and revenge on anyone who would come forward with identifying information. Werner also looked into the past of Zampogna, when he had served time in the penitentiary for receiving stolen goods. Werner thought perhaps this killing was an act of revenge for that occurrence. Because of the length of time since that occurred, Werner was able to discount this theory, as Zampogna had been engaged in legitimate business for the last several years. Despite semi-weekly ads in the local papers seeking information on the slaying, Werner was never able to secure enough information to solve the case

On August 21st, 1933, *The Ridgway Record* published a shocking story regarding a man who accused the State Police of kidnapping him concerning the Zampogna murder and holding him as a suspect. Frank Scopocaco of Johnsonburg had contacted the paper while he was receiving medical treatment at the Ridgway Hospital. According to Scopocaco, the State Police at Kane had "kidnapped" him off the streets of Johnsonburg and held him against his will for four days at the Kane State Police Station. Scopocaco said during that time; he was tortured and starved, even being denied water during his sustained interrogation. He was finally released on the fourth day, where he sought treatment at the Ridgway General Hospital.

Sergeant John Mullaney, Commanding officer of the Pennsylvania State Police at Kane, offered a rebuttal to Scopocaco's allegations. Mullaney termed Scopocaco's allegations "absurd" and declared his men were acting entirely within their rights as police authorities in holding Scopocaco for questioning. Mullaney further stated that Scopocaco was placed under arrest on suspicion and taken to the Kane Borough Jail where the officers investigated his story. The man was held in custody when his story conflicted with the stories of other witnesses. Scopocaco stated he was not near the scene of the Zampogna murder, while confidential sources claimed he was. Mullaney also stated that when they picked him up, Scopocaco went willingly with them to Kane, was given generous portions of food and water and was never tortured. He further stated that at no time during his detention did Scopocaco ask for his release, and he was released as soon as the investigation and questioning were completed. As far as taking the man out of the county without the knowledge of Elk County Detective Werner, he said the officers were acting entirely within their rights. The interrogation of Scopocaco never progressed further, and no charges were ever filed, by either the police or Scopocaco.

Despite a thorough and long-lasting investigation by Werner, an arrest for the murder of Joseph Zampogna proved elusive. Every tip the police received was followed up by strenuous investigations. The community in Johnsonburg was described as having a cloud descended upon it when it came to this murder. Although the detective more than likely correctly labeled this a "revenge" killing and not a gangland slaying, he would find no corresponding evidence with which to prove this. A legend still exists in Johnsonburg that some of the bullets fired through the body of Zampogna are lodged in the brick wall surrounding the house on the corner of Blaine and Grant Streets. It is certainly plausible that this happened, given the direction the bullets would have traveled. What is for certain is that no one was ever brought to trial for this heinous killing, and the case was added to the cold case file by early the next year. This murder marked the end of the violent killings in Johnsonburg that were labeled gangland. Prohibition was repealed, and the Black Hand moved on to other ventures. One wonders what the young Zampogna would have achieved in the construction world had he lived to an old age.

Zampogna's monument in the Holy Rosary
Cemetery. He is buried behind it.

Josephine Colle

Josephine's burial place, high on the hill at the Saint Joseph's Cemetery in Force.

On Thursday morning, July 7th, 1927, Felix Colle of Caledonia was on a mission. A number of groundhogs had taken up residence under his barn. Colle, twenty-one years old and recently married, decided he was going to end the life of these intruders and positioned himself behind a stone fence at the rear of his property. He was armed with a shotgun, which was loaded with a pumpkin ball. Colle planned to eliminate as many of these pests as possible. As Colle noticed a groundhog emerge from under his barn, he carefully aimed with the loaded shotgun and fired his weapon. The pumpkin ball missed the groundhog but hit a rock next to the barn. Colle heard a loud scream and looked up to find his young wife lying prone on the ground, blood pouring out of a wound to the head. Colle immediately ran to the aid of his wife, but death was almost instantaneous. He notified the authorities of what had happened, and Elk County Detective Leo Werner and Elk County Coroner Dr. Luhr were soon on the scene. A coroner's jury, hastily formed by Dr. Luhr, with the assistance of Dr. Hays of Byrnedale, decided that this was an accidental death, reaching this decision entirely upon the testimony of the husband, Felix. Detective Werner, however, was not so sure this was the cause and reported that he would take the matter further.

Josephine Beldin Colle was born in Emporium in 1907. She was twenty years old in 1927 and had been married to Felix but a short time before her death. Josephine was described as a very beautiful young woman that looked forward to a long and happy life; sadly, this was never to happen. She was buried at the Saint Joseph Cemetery in Force on Saturday, July 9th, 1927.

Elk County Detective Werner, Corporal Schmidt and Private Backner of the State Police meanwhile were conducting their own investigation into the shooting. A rough sketch of the scene, as relayed to the authorities by Colle, showed that Josephine was in a direct line of fire from the shotgun, and Felix could not have missed seeing her as he stated. Werner also spoke with neighbors of the Colle's who stated that more than one round was fired, contradicting Felix's statement that only one round was fired. Werner also gathered evidence that Colle had a "sweetheart" in Saint Marys, and that Colle had allegedly asked her if she would marry him if he did away with his wife. Neighbors and friends of the Colle's also stated that their relationship was one of constant fighting. Werner took the same kind of gun and bullet and hit the same rock, and the bullet did not and could not take the course told by Colle. Werner had several people stand where Felix stated his wife was standing, and when Werner fired multiple pumpkin shells at the rock, none ricocheted as Colle had said, and none of the people who stood where Mrs. Colle was alleged to have been standing, were in the least afraid of getting hit by the shot.

On Monday, July the 11th, Detective Werner, accompanied by State Policemen Schmidt and Backer went to the place of Felix's employment, Jones Construction Company, which was then doing construction near the Temple Theatre in Saint Marys. After a lengthy discussion, Colle was arrested and taken to the County Jail. Colle was reportedly calm and answered all questions put to him in a straight forward manner.

A hearing was held on Saturday, July 16th, in Saint Marys, to decide if the State's case against Felix Colle would go to the next term of court, with Justice Zelt presiding. D. J. Driscoll appeared for the defendant, while B. F. Ely, in the absence of District Attorney Straub, appeared for the Commonwealth. The state contended that Colle had made statements to the effect that his short-married life was beset with trouble at every turn and he wished to end it and marry a Saint Marys girl instead. The girl, Mary Cashmer, appeared for the Commonwealth at the hearing and stated that Colle had proposed marriage to her on several occasions. She told him she would not consider his proposal as long as he was married. Cashmer also testified that she visited Colle at the local hospital when he was a patient there, following an accident on the South Saint Marys Street paving job where he was employed. Colle once again asked her to marry him. Alois Sporner, of Saint Marys, who was a patient in the same ward as Colle at the hospital, said that Colle had asked him how to go about getting rid of his wife if he wanted to marry another girl. Sporner said he told him that such a procedure was against both the civil law and the law of the church. The Commonwealth also presented the reconstructive evidence that the incident could not have happened as Colle stated, as Josephine Colle had to have been in direct line of fire to receive the fatal wound and not as a result of a ricochet as Felix had stated. The case was bound over to the Court at this hearing, with Colle being held without bail in the death of his wife. Mary Cashmer was, interestingly, also held under a $1,000 bail as a material witness. Colle was then transported back to the Elk County Jail to await trial.

On Thursday, October 13th, the trial of Felix Colle for the murder of his wife, Josephine Colle on July 7th, got underway in Ridgway. Judge Darr of Brookville was the presiding Judge, and Attorneys Dennis Driscoll and John Arnold of DuBois represented Felix Colle. Assistance District Attorney B. F. Ely represented the Commonwealth. The Commonwealth presented their theories of the killing and the tests they performed, regarding the improbability of the shooting as told by Colle. They also presented their theory of motive, this being the other woman. Dr. Leo Hays of Byrnedale was the only witness called, and he stated that the shotgun slug had entered the left temple of Josephine Colle and exited on the right side. Death was instantaneous. The Commonwealth then rested. The defense began by asking for a dismissal of all charges, as "corpus delicti" had not been proven. Judge Darr, after a short wait, agreed with the defense and gave the jury binding instructions to find a verdict of not guilty, as the Commonwealth had no foundation for the charge of murder and evidence was only circumstantial at best. The jury then rendered a "not guilty" verdict. Felix Colle was immediately released from custody a free man.

Felix Colle denied he killed his wife for the rest of his life. He remained working in the Bennett's Valley area for some time after the shooting and never did marry Mary Cashmer. He ended up moving to a nearby community in 1931, where he married and fathered six children. He died of cancer in 1964. Detective Werner always stuck by his supposition that the shooting of Josephine was intentional, but the evidence was certainly lacking to provide any such conviction.

Obsession

Obsession and possession is how the story wore out in James City in 1920. Human history has revealed an inordinate number of stories of love gone astray and of love unrequited. This murder was one of obsession. An ex-husband was so infatuated with his former wife that he would do anything to possess her once again. She, on the other hand, had moved on and was in no way accepting of her ex's affections. As the obsession grew, danger became more realistic, culminating in a horrific finale to one more quest to possess one who was no longer within his grasp.

Lawrence Chadic was a hard-working glass plant employee who lived in James City. He was born in the Austrian Hungarian Empire and had immigrated to this area to pursue his version of the American dream. Soon after arriving in New York City, Chadic connected with several relatives living in the Elk County area and soon after secured employment with the glass factory in James City. Glass company management described Lawrence as having a great work ethic, something often seen among the immigrants of that era. He was but twenty-six years old in 1920 and was known to shun alcohol. His distaste for alcohol derived from a harsh childhood, in which alcohol caused his family to suffer many financial and emotional hardships. Not too long after Chadic had secured employment, he came into the acquaintance of the recently divorced Mrs. Majinink. Mrs. Majinink, the mother of three young children, was described as a real beauty who had suffered under her previous marriage. The single mother was what the doctor had prescribed for Chadic at this time, so far away from his homeland, and seeking comfort and companionship to allay his lonely existence. The relationship between the two developed at a rapid speed, with Chadic calling her the fulfillment of his dreams. Chadic could not wait for the day when she would become his lawful wife and bear him his own children. The Majinink children also bonded with the young Chadic, receiving warmth and encouragement, something they had not experienced with their father. The fairytale romance progressed, and a wedding followed within three months of the couple's meeting. The wedding took place in Ridgway on April 10th, 1920 and the new couple, along with the Majinink children, took up residence at James City.

Stephen Majinink had married his wife in 1914, and three children had quickly joined the family. Majinink's prolific drinking marred the marriage, and many arguments had taken place over their short but tumultuous union. Majinink had often threatened his wife with death should she leave him. Majinink had trouble holding down a long-term job due to his alcoholism. He went out West in search of employment. He was originally from Ottaway, Illinois, and he figured he would be able to secure employment in that area and then send for his family after he was settled. Mrs. Majinink wasted no time in filing for a divorce from her husband and went to the Elk County Courthouse to begin proceedings, citing cruel and unusual punishment as the reason. She then proceeded to move into her parents' home in James City, where her father kept a watchful eye over her and her children. When Stephen was served with the divorce papers, he became enraged and immediately headed back to James City from Illinois. He first tried to sweet talk his wife into getting back together and canceling the divorce proceedings. When Mrs. Majinink refused, he began to threaten her with death. He also threatened to kill their children and her parents, unless she came back to him. Mrs. Majinink, bolstered by her family and her circle of friends, rebuffed his advances and proceeded with the divorce. When Majinink made the death threats to his wife in front of law enforcement, he practically ended any chance of gaining custody of his children. In the November 1919 term of Elk County Court, Mrs. Majinink was awarded not only the divorce but also sole custody of her three children. Mr. Majinink was also ordered to stay away from his now ex-wife, but in those days, protection from abuse orders did not exist, and when he was caught in James City, he was just given a verbal warning to leave. Majinink eventually moved to Warren where he had secured employment, still full of rage. He kept in touch with friends from James City, who fed him information about the happenings of his ex-wife. He vowed to seek revenge, and when he found out that his ex-wife had taken a new love interest and was going to get married again, he set his murderous plan into action.

Majinink moved to Kane so he could be closer to his ex. He began to make sojourns into James City and quickly found the man whom his lost love had married. For over a month, he stalked Lawrence Chadic. Chadic, who never met Majinink, related to his wife that he thought he was being followed. He said that when he alighted from their house in the morning, he often noticed a strange man standing in the woods, observing his movements. He also noticed that when he came home, he often saw the same man following him in the streets of James City. His wife asked him to describe the man, and when he did, she knew it was her ex-husband. This brought fear in the Chadic household, and Mrs. Chadic informed the authorities in Elk County. The authorities told her they could not keep an armed guard on her house, but that the family should be alert at all times and to naturally report any further sightings of Majinink. Unfortunately, fate would intervene before law enforcement could do anything to protect the Chadic's.

Stephen Majinink chose August 13th, 1920, as the day he would seek revenge. This also happened to be Friday the 13th. Whether he chose this because of the symbolism or as a random date was never disclosed. He secured a .32 pistol and went to the Chadic residence in James City. He waited in the woods just outside of the backdoor of the residence. He knew from previous stalkings that Lawrence Chadic left for work at the glass plant at six in the morning. As the morning mist was lifting, Chadic appeared at the backdoor as usual. Majinink swiftly approached Chadic and immediately fired his pistol. Three bullets entered the body of Chadic, one entering the bicep muscles of the right arm and passing through the arm into the chest, piercing the lungs. A second bullet plowed into the victim's abdomen, while the third pierced his thigh. Chadic screamed out in pain and crumbled to the ground. Majinink immediately disappeared into the woods.

Mrs. Chadic heard the gunshots and her husband's screams of pain. She went to the back door and found her wounded spouse bleeding profusely and clutching his stomach. In terror, she went to the neighbors to seek help and told them to get transportation to the hospital in Kane as her husband was seriously injured. She then went back to comfort her husband. She could see the seriousness of his wounds and went into the house to get dressings for his wounds and a pillow to prop him up while they waited for transportation. Lawrence told her it was her ex-husband who did the deed. Within ten minutes, a company vehicle arrived, and Lawrence was transported to the Kane Summit Hospital. Mrs. Chadic accompanied her husband and reportedly never left his side during his short time there. Chadic, wounded in the lungs and abdomen, was given a dire prognosis and a surgeon was summoned from Ridgway to perform surgery.

Lawrence suffered in extreme pain until one o'clock in the afternoon, when he succumbed to his wounds. The now widow Chadic was heartbroken and could not be consoled. The man she had waited for, the man who showed her that true love had existed, was no more. Elk County Coroner Wilson convened a quick inquest and determined death was due to homicide by the hands of one Stephen Majinink. An arrest warrant was issued for Stephen Majinink, and a description was wired to local law enforcement officials to be on the lookout for the suspect. This initial description was to prove fateful in the proceeding days. Chadic's body was taken to the Brown Funeral Parlor in Kane and after a mass at St. Callistus Catholic Church; he was buried in the parish cemetery.

The manhunt began in the woods surrounding James City. The acquaintances of Majinink gave the authorities the following description of the suspect. He wore a dark suit of clothes, blue shirt, string tie, is of slim stature, has a scar on forehead, dark eyes, big lips, lame in one leg and is bow-legged. Elk County Deputy Sheriff Joseph May, Burgess Wood, and Officer Robinson traveled to Ludlow to search for the suspect after the search of the woods around James City proved fruitless. While in Ludlow at the train station, they observed a man acting strangely and placed the man into protective custody to determine if he was the suspect. The man emphatically denied having anything to do with the murder and complained about being detained. When searching the man, the authorities found a train ticket to Erie in his pockets. After telegraphing James City again about the description of the suspect, they found that their "suspect" did not have a scar on his forehead and also did not have bow legs. His clothing was also not the same as in the description. The authorities were satisfied that this man was not the suspect and released him from custody. According to Burgess Wood, the man "beat it as fast as his legs would carry him." This caused the arresting officers to gather the opinion that they may have had the correct suspect after all and perhaps the description of the killer was wrong. They momentarily began to pursue the stranger once again but were unable to find a trace of him. As the authorities knew that the man had a train ticket to Erie, they alerted the authorities in Erie to be on the lookout for a man with the revised description. "Wearing a blue coat, khaki shirt, string tie, stiff hat and with no scar on his forehead and not bow-legged." The original description, of a scar on the forehead and bow-legged, had caused the criminal to escape the hands of justice.

Majinink meanwhile was running for his life. Having narrowly escaped arrest, he flagged down the first automobile he saw in Ludlow. The auto was driven by a Bernal Connelly, who was driving to Warren. Majinink asked the gentleman for a lift to Warren and Connelly complied. During the drive to Warren, Majinink remarked to Connelly that he "had some trouble in James City." Connelly had not heard of the murder and only went to authorities after reading about the murder in the *Warren Times Observer*, after dropping Majinink off at the Warren National Bank. Majinink flagged down another auto heading towards Jamestown and alighted there. He then took the trolley route from Jamestown to Westfield and walked from the trolley station to Erie and the train depot. The Erie police, with the correct description, somehow allowed Majinink to purchase a train ticket to Lorain, Ohio and also allowed the suspect to board the New York Central Train headed in that direction. As the authorities had previously surmised that their suspect would be heading to Illinois, his former home, they had wired the description to all of the train stations between Erie and Illinois. When the train arrived in Lorrain, Ohio, the authorities were waiting, and quickly and quietly they took Majinink into custody.

The Lorrain, Ohio Police, on August 17th, wired the Elk County Sheriff's office that they had the suspect in custody and that they would hold him until they arrived. Deputy Sheriff May took the next train from Ridgway to Ohio. Majinink gave Deputy May no trouble as he was transported back to the Elk County Jail. During the train ride, Majinink spoke freely about what he had done and how he had escaped justice, even though it was for but a short time. May did recognize Majinink as the suspect they had detained in Ludlow, and the suspect confirmed it was he. Majinink told May the story of how he had hitched a ride to Warren and his travels to Erie. He said that at the Erie train station, he had passed right through the police officers stationed in the depot, and they had given him nary a glance. He suspected they had the wrong description, much like the one that had got him released in Ludlow. He felt a sense of invincibility and was shocked when he was arrested in Ohio. Majinink also confessed to the shooting and said his emotions got the best of him. He swore he loved his former spouse and could not stand to be away from her and his children. He expressed remorse and said he was ready to take whatever punishment came his way. He was questioned as to the weapon he had used to shoot Chadic. Majinink state he used a "short gun" to commit the murder. When questioned further as to the whereabouts of the gun, Majinink said he threw it in the woods this side of James City. When asked if he would lead them to the weapon, Majinink replied that he could not do it, as he could not remember just where he threw it and did not want to see it again.

Majinink was arraigned and placed in the Elk County Jail without bail. J. H. Thompson, esquire, of Saint Marys was appointed as his defense attorney. The case was scheduled for trial in the October 1920, term of Court. Judge R. B. McCormick, special presiding Judge from Lock Haven, was the court master. Majinink made a full confession to authorities and waived a jury trial. He appeared in the Court on October 5th, 1920 and was sentenced by Judge McCormick to not less than six nor more than seven years in the Western Penitentiary. Majinink served his time, and his whereabouts after the prison sentence is not known. His former wife was said to have remarried once again and left James City for good. Chadic's family back in Austria-Hungary were informed of his demise but never were able to travel to his final resting place to pay their respects.

Hallton Hell

Hallton, around the time of the murder.

Spring Creek Township was dotted with lumber camps in the earlier parts of the twentieth century. Some of the lumbering operations in existence were the Portland Lumber Company, Horton Crary & Company, G. W Rhines, Hall & Kaul and the Empire Lumber companies to name a few. These lumber camps employed many men to perform the intense physical operations. The majority of these jobs were filled by recent immigrants to the Country, with the majority coming from Europe. Lumber camps back in those days had sizable populations of Italians, Germans, Swedes, Poles, and Slavs who had traveled to the area to find work and start their quest to the American dream. Within each lumber camp was also a kind of mini-village, where men from similar origin often stuck together and did not mix with the others who came from different parts of Europe. These mini-communities spoke their native languages, and not only worked together but partied together. Many times, these "parties" or celebrations got out of hand, and physical fights arose. The battles were often forgotten when the men woke up from their alcoholic slumber and the enemies of the night before, became comrades in arms once again.

One of these ethnic lumber camps was located near the hamlet of Hallton back in 1911. The camp was occupied by the usual smattering of Italians and Poles, and a number of Austrians. Ludwig Probatz was a recent immigrant from the Austrian Hungarian Empire. He had been in America for about two years in 1911 and had worked almost exclusively in the lumber industry. He was known as a hard worker and a hard drinker. Probatz, who was unmarried, had no known family in the United States and instead spent his free time with his fellow countrymen. Tony or "Joe" Vicic was also from the Austrian Hungarian Empire. The pair had become quick friends and spent their free time drinking and reminiscing of the land they left behind. Vicic was also a single man in 1911. Probatz and Vicic were known to carouse together often and were both anticipating the upcoming 4th of July Holiday. The two Austrians, while not yet American Citizens, anticipated claiming citizenship in the near future, and thoroughly enjoyed celebrating this, the most patriotic holiday of American Independence. As the 4th of July fell upon a Tuesday in 1911, the duo planned to celebrate on Saturday, the 2nd of July, as neither had to work on Sunday. The men went into the village of Hallton and were seen drinking and celebrating at the local tavern. The men continued to drink into the early evening when a fight erupted between the heavily intoxicated countrymen. The duo was escorted out of the tavern and told not to come back that evening. The men, realizing they had lost their source of alcohol by getting thrown out of the bar, decided they would have to retire to their quarters, where they had a bottle of alcohol hidden, to continue their celebrating. The men also settled their differences and were seen walking arm in arm on their way back to their lumber camp.

A rule in these lumber camps was that no alcohol was to be kept upon the premises. The proprietors of the lumber mills knew that alcohol was the cause of many fights, as well as a decrease in productivity. Most of the men followed this rule and only imbibed in alcohol when they went to town on the weekends. The men returned worse for wear on Saturday nights, but after recovering on Sundays, they were reenergized on the following Monday and ready for the work week.

Probatz and Vicic returned to their camp around six in the evening and Vicic retrieved the bottle of alcohol he had hidden in his trunk. The men continued to drink, and in short order, the prior argument developed once again. The two men, now extremely intoxicated, began to quarrel and blows were struck. In the heat of the battle, Vicic secured an iron bar he found on the floor and hit Probatz over the back of the head, causing Probatz to fall to the floor unconscious. Vicic, realizing what he had done sobered up immediately. He attempted to arouse his countryman, and when he found this impossible, he plotted his escape. He first bandaged Probatz's head with a rag and placed a pillow under his head. Vicic then emptied his trunk, and with his possessions in tow, he made his escape, without alerting anyone to his misdeed.

The living quarters of lumber camps were wooden barracks which held between six or more occupants, with bunks as the sleeping arrangements. Each laborer had a small personal space where they were given a trunk to store their possessions. In the lumber camp of Vicic and Probatz, they shared their barracks with six other countrymen who were not present when the fight took place. When his fellow bunkmates returned at a later hour, they found Probatz in a critical condition, and they immediately had the camp foreman arrange transportation to the Elk County General Hospital in Ridgway. The journey over the primitive road to Ridgway took over an hour, and when Probatz arrived at the hospital, he was given a dire prognosis. Probatz lingered on at the hospital for two days, succumbing to his injuries on the 4th of July 1911, never having regained consciousness. The coroner ruled the death as a homicide due to a fracture of the vault of the skull which caused "meningitis" to set in. The authorities, already searching for Vicic, were informed of Probatz's death and the assault investigation became a homicide investigation.

Vicic had meanwhile not been seen since the day of the attack. The Elk County Detective had spent considerable time in Hallton and the surrounding lumber camps and had received no reliable information of Vicic's present location. Many of the lumber camp inhabitants refused to speak with the authorities, fostering long-held beliefs, that the authorities could not be trusted. These beliefs had transferred from the old countries, which were ruled by absolute monarchies, and where authority was always treated with suspicion. The trail of Vicic quickly turned cold, and the authorities admitted they had no idea of the whereabouts of the accused.

Probatz's body was prepared for burial by the Van Aken Funeral Home in Ridgway. He was thought to have been approximately forty-five years of age. As he had no known family in the area, the cost of burial was borne by the Elk County Commissioners. His burial took place in the pauper's field, which was located adjacent to the established cemeteries and located on Montmorenci Road in Ridgway. A search of Probatz's trunk in the lumber camp had found a number of letters from Austria that he had received from his family. A translator wrote a letter of sympathy to the family back in Austria, and this is the last correspondence that ever took place between the family in Austria. Today Probatz lies in an unmarked grave, far from his homeland.

The last that this case was mentioned was in September of 1911. "The Elk County Commissioners offered a reward of $250 for the detention and or apprehension and conviction of Tony Vicic alias Joe Vicic. Vicic had a warrant in which he was charged with the murder of Ludwig Probatz. Tony Vicic was described as an Austrian, about thirty-five years of age; weight about one hundred eighty-four pounds, five feet six inches tall, small mustache and sandy complexion. According to the reward announcement, "for some time past the Elk County Officials have had a clue as to the whereabouts of the assailant of Probatz and have been quietly watching his movements. It is thought that the reward will stimulate interest and it is expected an arrest will likely be made within the next week." This press release was most certainly a ruse to get Vicic or those that knew of his whereabouts to turn him in. It would have been unbelievable that the authorities would have been watching the movements of Vicic in quiet, while he was meanwhile wanted for murder. One theory at the time was that he had traveled to another lumber camp within the tri-county area and changed his name. Leads were followed up and a detective visited each and every camp to question the supervisors as to if they had seen Vicic or perhaps had heard of his present location. This investigation found no credible information on the whereabouts of Vicic, and he was never found. Theories of his location ranged from that he moved to parts unknown in the United States and continued his employment, to some reports that he returned to the old country and lived the rest of his life, knowing that he caused a man's death due to his love of the bottle.

Chicken Feed

Mary Nulf's grave, next to her husband in the Brockport Cemetery.

The James Nulf family of Brockport had a typical outward appearance as being one of harmony and happiness. James had married late in life at the age of fifty-one, to Mary Johnson, who was some nineteen years, his junior. In the ten years since their marriage, they had been blessed with two sons, James Jr., and Charles. Mr. Nulf was described as having been a man of means, and also a keen shot, having been known to make successful shots at deer from long distances. All who knew him said he was of a temperate nature and none had known him to have a temper. It was however known, that Nulf was a miserly man, who often would argue over a bill to get it reduced at every chance he could. Mary, on the other hand, was described as a very conscientious mother who put the well-being of her family first and had recently moved her elderly mother, Mrs. Charlotte Johnson, into her house to care for her, as she could no longer care for herself. Mrs. Johnson, seventy-six years old, was no longer mobile on her own and had to be assisted wherever she ventured. As the outward appearance of this family portrayed one of quiet bliss, one must wonder what was hidden behind the closed doors. The actions of Mr. Nulf on both the fateful day and the day previous were something that appeared to have been way out of character. What type of evil visited the Nulf family in December of 1926?

On Wednesday, December 29th, 1926, Mrs. Mary Nulf was completing her household chores as usual. With the recent Christmas Holiday passed, she was preparing for the New Years and with the recent addition of her elderly mother to her house; she now had another person dependent on her care, besides her two young sons. As school was not in session, her boys were home and busily playing with the toys they had received from Christmas. Mary had finished serving lunch to her family when she went outside to feed the chickens and other animals the family kept. When Mary entered the barn, she found that the chicken feed had frozen solid during the night and she was unable to scoop out enough to feed the ever-hungry chickens. She decided to carry the bag into the kitchen to thaw out; planning to take the bag back to the barn after the feed had loosened up. Mary placed the bag of feed next to the stove in her kitchen and went on with her other chores. While Mary was washing the dishes from lunch, her husband entered the kitchen. He noticed the feed bag next to the stove and inquired about his wife as to what was it doing in the house? When Mary explained that the feed was frozen, and she was thawing it out, without warning, James struck her in the side of the face with his fist.

This unexpected attack caused Mrs. Nulf to fall to the kitchen floor. Nulf said never to bring the chicken feed into the house again. James then went up the stairs to his bedroom, while Mrs. Nulf's oldest son attended to his mother. The side of Mrs. Nulf's face was extremely bruised, and she also suffered a swollen lip. Several of her teeth were also loosened due to the severity of the blow she received. Mrs. Nulf brushed herself off and checked herself in the mirror to see her appearance. Her face was beginning to become purple and red and was horribly puffed up. With several teeth being loose, she knew she needed to visit the local dentist for assistance the next day. Mrs. P. M. Cuneo, a neighbor, had stopped in later that afternoon and found Mrs. Nulf crying at the kitchen table, and in outright disbelieve that her husband had struck her over something as insignificant as chicken feed in the house. Mrs. Cuneo comforted her neighbor and took the chicken feed out to the barn and also fed the chickens. Cuneo also reported that Mr. Nulf had entered the kitchen while she was visiting and that he had acted very cordially, ignoring the scene that Cuneo was presented with. Mrs. Cuneo later reported that this was the first time she had seen injuries on Mrs. Nulf inflicted by her husband. The rest of the evening, Mr. and Mrs. Nulf avoided conflict by remaining in separate rooms, and when it came time for bed, Mary slept in the spare bedroom with her mother, Charlotte. The rest of the night proved uneventful, with Mr. Nulf staying in his bedroom.

On Thursday, December 30th, Mrs. Nulf arose as usual at seven in the morning and helped her mother dress. She moved her mother to the kitchen table and went and aroused her children. She then began to prepare breakfast for the household, and her two sons joined their grandmother at the kitchen table. She yelled for her husband that breakfast was almost ready and that he should come down to eat. As she stood at the stove cooking, her husband entered the kitchen and exclaimed to his wife "have you had enough?" He then produced a shotgun he had hidden behind his back and fired the gun towards his wife without warning. The bullet, a one-ounce pumpkin ball, struck her in the upper part of the right arm, passing through the arm and into the shoulder where it continued through the lungs and came out through the upper part of the left chest and struck the chimney just behind the stove. After being shot, Mrs. Nulf staggered a few feet to the door leading to the back porch, opened the door and fell on her face onto the porch where she died within a few moments, her body lying in a pool of blood. Mrs. Nulf was able to loudly scream for help before she expired, and this brought some of the neighbors running to the Nulf house.

The neighbors gathered around Mrs. Nulf's body, lying on the back porch with the door opened into the kitchen. The neighbors said that Mr. Nulf was smiling and told the neighbors that he would shoot the first person that tried to enter his house. The neighbors implored him to let them remove the body of Mrs. Nulf, whom they believed was still alive, but Nulf repeated his threat and told them to leave, or they too would die. He then pointed his shotgun directly at the neighbors, and they scattered, worried that he would carry out his threat. As the group was fleeing, they heard Nulf laugh out loud in a sinister way. The authorities in Brockway and Ridgway were notified by the neighbors of this tragic incident.

Brockway Chief of Police Bloom and Dr. George Humphreys were the first on the scene. They spoke with the neighbors and approached the back porch of the Nulf residence with caution, as they were told of the threats the neighbors had received. Stepping over the deceased body of Mrs. Nulf, Chief Bloom could see Mrs. Nulf's mother seated at the kitchen table, unable to remove herself from the scene and her face revealed an expression of horror. The two young Nulf children were seated next to her, silently crying, lest their father return and carry out the threats he had made to them. Chief Bloom motioned for the young Nulf children to exit the residence and they did at once. Bloom then entered the kitchen and questioned the elderly Mrs. Johnson. The house was eerily quiet which added to the danger of the situation. Mrs. Johnson, who spoke little English, motioned to Bloom that the perpetrator had retreated upstairs. Bloom ascended the stairs, followed closely by some of the male neighbors who were also now armed. At the top of the stairs, Bloom found the door to the bedroom closed. He knocked at the door several times, but no answer was forthcoming. Bloom decided to break down the door and perhaps surprise Mr. Nulf. Upon breaking down the door, Bloom was greeted with the prone body of Nulf, lying on his back with glassy eyes turned up towards the ceiling and with a gaping hole in his breast. Dr. Humphreys later surmised that Nulf had climbed onto his bed and rested the trigger of the shotgun against the foot of the bed, placed the muzzle against his chest and with a ramrod, had pressed the trigger, death being almost instantaneous. His body had then tumbled off the bed, where Chief Bloom found it.

Within a couple of hours, Elk County Sheriff John Halter, Deputy Sheriff May, Elk County Detective Leo Werner, Elk County District Attorney G. B. Straub, and newspapermen from Ridgway and Saint Marys arrived on the scene. Elk County Coroner A. C. Luhr followed shortly. A detachment of State Policemen from Punxsutawney, armed with tear gas, were called back to their barracks, after discovering that the perpetrator was found dead in the house.

An unnamed newspaperman who accompanied Detective Werner gave the following account of what he had witnessed when he arrived: "Many motorists who have driven through Brockport may recall seeing the wooden, unpainted Catholic Church on the left-hand side of the road as you drive towards Brockway. Two doors beyond the church stands the house where today's tragedy occurred. Some little distance back from the road it gives every appearance of being well cared for. Its yellow paint gleamed brightly today against the contrasting white of the snow-covered ground. The front room, heated with a coal stove, was crowded with neighbors of the dead pair who gathered to give what solace they could to the aged Mrs. Johnson, and the two boys, James Jr., aged six and Charles four, orphaned by their father's rash deed. A door that refused to stay shut led into the kitchen and here on a couch laid the dead woman placed there by the hands of the first persons called to the scene. A boudoir cap was on her head, the uncombed hair peeking from beneath the cap's edges, the face slumped down in that attitude that bespeaks the begging of mercy. In the fleshy part of the upper right arm was a tear through the sleeve of the dress, black clotted blood at this point denoting the course the shot took as she fled towards the door hoping to escape the wrath of a madman. Upstairs was the man who had caused her death...himself a victim of the same gun that had thundered its doom to the woman."

The Nulf children, as well as the aged Mrs. Johnson, were removed from the scene and neighbors took them into town where they were placed with relatives.

The gathered authorities then began to piece together the tragic and appalling tragedy that had engulfed the normally peaceful hamlet of Brockport. Coroner Luhr, after examining the bodies of the two dead persons, quickly impaneled a jury composed of the following people, some of whom accompanied him to the residence. H. A. Thompson of Ridgway, foreman, J. J. Luhr, Alfred Straub, H. T. Obrien of Saint Marys, Reverend P. C. Heilbrien of Brockway and John S. Halter of Johnsonburg.

Chief of Police Bloom was called as a witness and told of being summoned to the home and of finding Mrs. Nulf on the back porch. He also stated that he went inside in search of Nulf and discovered him lying dead in his bedroom.

Mrs. P. M. Cuneo, the neighbor, told about visiting the Nulf home the preceding afternoon and finding Mrs. Nulf's face swollen and bruised and she had been crying. Mrs. Nulf had told Cuneo about the argument and the beating administered by her husband. Cuneo testified that Nulf was in the room when she arrived and spoke very cordially to her, not in any way intimating that anything was wrong.

Dr. George Dumphries, the family physician, was the next witness and he said that Nulf had borne a very good reputation as did Mrs. Nulf. He knew of nothing wrong with Nulf mentally.

After a short deliberation, the jury returned with the following verdict: "That Mrs. James Nulf came to her death at the hands of her husband, who shot her with a 12-gauge shotgun and death was not accidental. Also, that James Nulf came to his death at his own hands by a self-inflicted bullet wound." The case was then ruled closed unless any further information was uncovered that would substantially change the ruling.

James Nulf was survived by a sister and brother who both lived in Brockport, as well as the two children he had with his deceased wife. Mrs. Nulf was survived by not only her children but by her aged mother and a sister and two brothers. The Nulf's were buried side by side in the Brockport Cemetery.

The cause of this homicide is especially troublesome. A fight over something as insignificant as chicken feed points to there being a far more underlying problem in the Nulf household. As Mrs. Cuneo, the neighbor testified, she had never seen Mrs. Nulf as a victim of physical abuse prior to the murder. To commit such a ghastly murder in front of not only one's mother-in-law but in front of his two young children is appalling. No sane person would ever consider this action, whether or not it was done in the throes of passion, which it was not. As the certificate of death of Mr. Nulf recorded death due to a self-inflicted shot through the heart as the cause of death, no further tests on his body were conducted. I am pretty sure that if an autopsy of James Nulf's brain was conducted, a tumor would have been found, which would have better explained this tragedy. As this was not done, no explanation could be given, except that Mr. Nulf suffered from a temporary fit of madness. It was also interesting to read the newspaperman's account of the crime scene being overrun by neighbors and strangers, all allowed to have, what appears to have been unfettered access right under the very eyes of law enforcement. Although this was most certainly a case of murder and suicide, one wonders if all of the murder scenes which took place during this era were also compromised?

Missing in Highland

The Old Lamont Road in Highland Township where Edwin
Adams was last seen back in 1910.

Of all the cases I have researched, this is the most mysterious
and I would submit, the scariest one of the whole lot. The
disappearance of nine-year-old Edwin Adams from Lamont, in
Highland Township back in 1910, has all the details of child
abduction. As I have a camp in Highland, I have spent hours
roaming those woods, and the circumstances of this case stay in
my mind every time I explore the area.

On Saturday afternoon, April 16th, 1910, nine-year-old Edwin Adams of Lamont, Arthur Mahoney, Arthur Williams, and Orville Young decided to go fishing on Wolf Run which was located on the Old Lamont road. The day was unseasonably warm, and the boys had the fishing "itch," after having spent a long and cold winter holed up with what is described as cabin fever. Edwin's father had told him earlier in the week that a game warden was in the area, and that to be careful of getting caught on private property if they went out fishing. The head end of Wolf run was on private property, and Edwin shared with his friends that there was a game warden spotted in the area and that they should be on the lookout. The boys spent the afternoon catching some native trout and catching up on stories from each of their prospective households. At around four o'clock, the boys were startled when a strange man emerged from the heavy pines that surrounded the stream and stood and stared at them. The boys screamed at his sudden appearance, and all of them took off through the woods towards Lamont. As three of the boys were aged from twelve to fourteen years, they naturally were able to run faster than little Edwin. They stopped when they reached the first house on the old Lamont Road and waited for Edwin to catch up. After Edwin did not appear for half an hour, they decided to seek help, as they all were too afraid to go back into the woods to search for Edwin. They went to Edwin's parent's house and told his father and mother what had happened. Mr. Adams, who was the supervisor of the United Natural Gas Company in Lamont, went to the company barracks and aroused all of his employees. The men, numbering in the area of twenty-five, followed the boys to the exact spot that Edwin was last seen. They all spread out in different directions and constantly bellowed out the youngster's name. Word was sent to Kane that a young boy was lost in the woods, and Chief of Police Ives organized another search party of around one hundred men and headed out towards Lamont.

The men searched the woods and fields throughout the Lamont area during the night, but no trace of Edwin was found. A steady rain began to fall around midnight, and the search was called off, with plans to start the search in earnest at the first light.

At dawn on Sunday morning, April the 17th, the growing search party met at the gas plant and made plans for the search. The group from Kane was now joined by a search party from the neighboring towns of Wilcox, Johnsonburg, Saint Marys, and Ridgway, which Elk County Sheriff Hacherl had hastily organized. The total search party numbered close to three hundred men and grew throughout the day with additional communities sending volunteers. A local man also brought a bloodhound to aid in the search. As the forests of Lamont were crisscrossed with pipelines and roads, the searchers all felt that the boy would emerge on one of these open areas. The men planned a grid search for each area, and the search went on from sunrise to sundown with no success. The bloodhound picked up the boy's trail where his companions had last saw him, but the hound only went six hundred feet into the woods and lost the scent. The handler said it was as if the boy was picked up at this point by someone or something. As the day progressed, the rain turned to freezing rain and then to snow.

Mr. Adams had informed his employer, Superintendent Craig, of Buffalo, New York, of his misfortune, and Craig had offered the full resources of his company. Some three hundred employees of the gas company headed towards Lamont from various plants, to aid in the search, arriving late at night on Sunday. Mr. Craig also employed Mr. Charles E. Weeks, of Buffalo, who had a pack of three trained bloodhounds, and they too arrived with the Buffalo party. The Pennsylvania State Police were also alerted, and they made plans to send fifty horse mounted troopers on Monday morning.

As the situation in Lamont was developing, reports were received from Ludlow, eighteen miles from Lamont, that a seven-year-old boy had disappeared on the same day as young Edwin and in mysteriously the same type of situation. Young Michael Steffan had accompanied another young boy out fishing in a stream near his house and had disappeared when his friend rounded a bend in the creek. Search parties were also combing the streams and woods of Ludlow with the same result as in Lamont. Eight hours separated these two disappearances.

On Monday morning, April the 17th, the search began once again. The now over four hundred searchers were joined by the fifty mounted State Police Officers. The police rode their horses at arm's length through each of the search grids that had been established, and sources figured that over eight square miles were covered on Monday alone. The bloodhounds picked up the trail of the boy at the point where he was last seen, and these highly trained dogs, who had found many a missing person in the past, went only six hundred feet into the woods and then lost the trail as the prior hound had. Their owner, Mr. Weeks, declared that he was certain that the boy was picked up at this spot and removed from the area. No sign of the boy was found on Monday either. The party was also joined by a group of some three hundred New York prison inmates, who had volunteered their services, after hearing of the disappearance. Many of these searchers split their time between Lamont and Ludlow in their fruitless task. The physical search of the woods went on for the rest of the week with no success.

The authorities began to think of different scenarios in these disappearances. In Lamont, there was a large pond that was used in the gas company operations. Some thought it possible that the young Edwin may have somehow fallen into the pond and drowned. The pond was dragged on Monday, and no trace of Edwin was found. The stream Edwin had disappeared on was too small to hide a body, so while the stream was searched, there was no need to drag it. The streams in Ludlow were much deeper, and the authorities did drag these bodies of water, also without success.

The detectives also grilled the other boys as to the description of the man that they saw. All of the boys seemed to be suffering from shock and neither could nor would offer much information. The police offered theories to the youngsters that maybe they hurt or accidentally killed young Edwin and perhaps hid his body to cover up their misdeed. The boys vehemently denied these allegations and held steadfast to the story that a strange man had appeared, and that was the last they saw of Edwin. The theory of the boys having anything to do with the disappearance was discounted when no sign of Edwin was found in the many areas searched.

As news spread throughout Pennsylvania and New York, tips began to pour in. One particular tip caught law enforcement's eyes. A merchant from Red House, Cattaraugus County, New York, named Mr. McCabe, phoned the State Police and told a most interesting tale. McCabe said that when he boarded the train on Saturday night, the 16th, at Red House, headed towards Salamanca, he had observed a man seated with a young boy. The boy cried profusely throughout the journey and continued to cry when McCabe had alighted at Salamanca. McCabe, who was unaware of the disappearance on the Saturday that he observed this, had only recollected this event when he read a newspaper account of the missing boy. McCabe said the boy resembled the description of the lost boy described in the article. The authorities knew that the train stopped at Kinzua, which could easily have been reached by a man carrying a young boy from Lamont in time to get on the train and then to have been observed on Saturday night heading towards Salamanca. The train route ended in Olean, New York, and the authorities contacted the police there to have them get in contact with the conductor, to find out if he knew where the man and boy had gone. In a strange twist of fate, Mr. Craig, the superintendent of the gas works that employed young Edwin's father, also was on the train on Saturday night heading towards Olean and eventually Buffalo. Craig stated that he too saw the boy, but the boy was not over four years of age and bore no resemblance to Edwin. This lead was eventually discounted.

A mass meeting was held in Kane on Tuesday evening in which more than five hundred men and boys appeared and volunteered their services. This large group of searchers joined the already massive number of men in Lamont, and they walked in lines over miles and miles of terrain on Wednesday with no results for their effort. The Authorities continued searching the area around Lamont for another week, but as the weather began to reach below zero at night, they knew there was practically no chance the boy would be found alive if he even was in the area.

The authorities now decided that this was a kidnapping, a theory that was entertained before, but something they could not fathom as happening in such a rural and sparsely inhabited area. A theory of a kidnapping for ransom was also discussed, but as no ransom note was forthcoming and as the Adam's family was not well off, this theory was discarded. As the authorities were scratching their heads, they accepted all types of tips and assistance that was offered. A "clairvoyant" from Pittsburgh, Mrs. Lewis, offered her services. An article of Edwin's clothing was delivered to her in Pittsburgh. She said she could not see the location of the child, but that the Adams boy was alive, but receiving cruel treatment. She was of the opinion that the boy was in the hands of foreigners. Foreigners at that time meant those who could not speak English. Following up on any lead, the authorities then began to visit the houses of foreign speaking people throughout the area and searched their houses looking for any sign of the boy. This was also not successful.

The searches for the Adams and Steffan boys continued for three weeks non-stop, and on the weekends, the number of searchers was over one thousand men and boys. The parties switched between Lamont and Ludlow and the area searched widened with each coming day. The only "clue" that was found in this time period was a note, that was fastened to a trestle along Wolf Run, discovered on May the 2nd by Carl Tew. The note said, "Your Boy will be returned for $10,000." On the reverse side of the note, it simply said: "Leave Reward." The note was turned over to the State Police, who had taken over the investigation, and was eventually dismissed as a cruel joke.

Eventually, the search parties wound down, and the Lamont and Kane communities got back to normality. The Adam's family never gave up hope that their son was alive and would someday come back home. Nothing was ever heard of from either Edwin or the Steffan child ever since that fateful day in April. There are too many similarities in these stories for them not to have been connected. It is almost certain that the Adam's boy was abducted shortly after he was last seen and carried far out of the area for some nefarious reason. The Steffan boy could more easily have drowned in the stream he was fishing on, as the river was over twenty feet wide in some places and some of the holes were known to be quite deep. I tend to believe that since the body was never found in the waters and since not only did he disappear, but his fishing pole and gear also disappeared, that the drowning was not a solution to the disappearance. Whatever happened on that April day back in 1910 will surely haunt the woods and fields of Highland for the rest of eternity.

That such a deed could have occurred in literally the middle of nowhere is indeed so troubling. Another troubling fact is that the surviving boys never gave a concise description of the "Strange Man." They only said his appearance was dark and "scary."

Wolf Run, on the Old Lamont Road, where the boys were fishing when Edwin disappeared.

Indian Giver

The Sawmill of N. L. Hoover located at Dahoga around the
time of the murder.

I am sure everyone has borrowed something from someone
at some time, as well as borrowed something out. Most times
the borrowed item has been returned with none the worse for
wear, but sometimes items are returned damaged. This latter
category has been known to cause quarrels and long-lasting
feuds between both friends and blood relatives. The worse
category is when something is never returned or returned after a
lengthy time. This is the story of one such incident, when an
item, as common as a trowel, was returned long after it was
borrowed and in a damaged state. Read how this simple trowel
caused a man's death and the loss of liberty for another man.

Ralph Manno of Dahoga was on a mission on October 14th,
1909. Mr. Manno was in a foul mood due to the constant
pestering of his countryman, Rocco Raffalo, for the return of a
trowel he had borrowed in the spring when he was doing
masonry work on his dwelling in Dahoga. Manno had carelessly

misplaced the tool amidst the project and would not admit to Raffalo that he lost the loaned item, nor would he offer to replace it. Raffalo was employed in the construction trade, and the loss of this implement was sorely missed. As spring turned to summer and summer turned to fall, Manno avoided Raffalo like the plague. Raffalo, who also lived in Dahoga, above Wilcox, would frequently stop at the Manno residence when he was passing and knock at the front door. Most of the times Mrs. Manno would answer, as her husband would hide if he was home. She would tell the desperate Raffalo that Mr. Manno was not at home and she had no idea where the trowel in question was. As Raffalo continued his visits and began to knock louder on the front door, Mrs. Manno became irate at these constant and harassing visits and started to become nasty to the unwanted visitor, with neighbors reporting foul language and insults erupting in Italian coming from the Manno residence whenever Raffalo visited. Mrs. Manno could no longer take the weekly interruptions in her life and deplored her husband to find the trowel or buy Raffalo a new one. Mr. Manno now had not only Raffalo, but also his wife on his back in regard to the misplaced trowel. Manno finally decided that he would find the trowel and return it to Raffalo. Manno spent the entire day searching through his basement and the shed in the back of his house and in the last place he searched, he found the trowel, exactly where he had placed it when he was finished with his job. The trowel was no longer pristine, having cement caked to the surface and also rusted from the elements. Manno decided to return the trowel as it was found, forgetting that the loan of the trowel was offered in friendship, but instead determined to make the trowel an object of a lifetime grudge. Manno yelled to his wife that he had found the trowel and that they would be traveling to the Raffalo residence that very evening to deliver it and put an end to this saga.

While Manno was looking for the trowel, a friend, Bruno Vavala (the same individual from Volume I), arrived at the Manno house to visit. Vavala accompanied Manno while he searched for the trowel that he needed to return to Raffalo. Vavala offered to accompany Manno to the Raffalo residence and they, accompanied by Mrs. Manno, set out towards the Raffalo residence. When they arrived at the Raffalo residence, they found he was not home and were told he was in the Village of Wilcox. The party set out towards Wilcox, and along the way, they passed a neighbor's house and saw Raffalo. Manno motioned for Raffalo to come to the sidewalk and presented the trowel. Raffalo grabbed the trowel and seeing its condition, loudly proclaimed that Manno was not even a human being and likened him to a "cesso" in Italian, which was an extreme insult, as the meaning was a toilet. The sidewalks in those days were very narrow and made out of wooden planks, similar to wooden pallets. As Raffalo turned to leave, he found Mrs. Manno was blocking his way and yelling that Raffalo was an unfit beast. Raffalo pushed her out of the way, and Mrs. Manno fell into the muddy road. Mr. Manno quickly pulled a pistol from his coat and shot Raffalo in the back of the head.

Raffalo crumpled to the sidewalk, death being instantaneous. The neighbors that Raffalo was visiting ran into Wilcox to inform Constable Doane of the shooting. The aged Constable George Doane was not too sure that he could handle the case by himself and he called Johnsonburg and notified Constable McClintic and Dr. Sharp of the shooting. Doane said he was going to Dahoga to apprehend Manno and would appreciate assistance. Doane took Manno into custody without resistance and lodged him in the small jail cell at Wilcox. The body of Raffalo was not disturbed from where he died. Constable McClintic, Dr. Sharp and several deputies arrived shortly and took over the crime scene. After interviewing the only direct witnesses to the shooting, Vavala and Mrs. Manno were taken to the Elk County Jail to be held as witnesses. The body of Raffalo was transported to Amend Funeral Parlor in Wilcox, where Dr. Sharp conducted a hastily formed coroner's inquest. Raffalo had died from a single bullet wound that had entered the base of his brain and which had fractured his spine. Death would have been instantaneous. The cause of death was ruled to be homicide by the hands of Ralph Manno. As the jail at Wilcox was not secure, nor meant for extended stays, Manno was transported to the Elk County Jail.

Rocco Raffalo was around thirty-three years of age in 1909. He was married and had two children, all of whom still lived in Italy. Raffalo was saving up for the day he would be able to have them come and live in America. He was employed in the local industries as a mason and also was a barber on the side. As he had no family in this country, a simple Catholic service was held over the remains, and his body was transported to the Catholic Cemetery in Rasselas for burial.

The trial of Ralph Manno, charged with the murder of Rocco Raffalo, commenced on Tuesday morning, January 5th, 1910, in the Elk County Courthouse. Judge Harry Alvin Hall presided with the Commonwealth represented by District Attorney McFarlin and D. J. Driscoll while the defendant was represented by E. H. Baird and John B. Whitmore. The first witness called was Dr. Sharp. Sharp testified to the wound that Raffalo received and that it was sufficient to cause death. As one of the only two eyewitnesses was Mrs. Manno, and she could not be called to testify against her husband, Bruno Vavala was the next witness. He testified to having witnessed the confrontation over the trowel and also said he saw Raffalo push Mrs. Manno. Vavala also testified that he heard words exchanged but could not hear them clearly and then he heard the shot and saw the pistol in Manno's hand. The prosecution then offered the pistol from the murder scene into the evidence. It was noted that the defense offered no objections to any of the evidence or facts of the case that the Commonwealth offered. Attorney Driscoll then rested the case for the Commonwealth.

Attorney J. G. Whitmore opened for the defense. Whitmore admitted to the jury that Manno had indeed shot Raffalo, but this was done in the act of self-defense. A razor was found in the dead man's pocket, and the defense offered this as evidence. Whitmore explained that Raffalo had displayed the razor while they were arguing and threatened to slice Manno's neck. When Raffalo pushed Mrs. Manno off of the narrow walkway, Manno believed Raffalo had stabbed her and drew and fired his weapon to prevent further stabbings. This was the premise of the defense.

Attorney Driscoll immediately attempted to quell the self-defense argument by admitting statements from the Dahoga residents that Raffalo, who worked in his spare time as a barber, had just finished up shaving a customer before Manno's visit. Raffalo had placed the razor in his pocket and had traveled to the store to finish making arrangements for bringing his wife to this country. On the way back from the store, Raffalo had happened upon Manno and the situation developed.

Attorney Whitmore then called numerous citizens of Dahoga and the surrounding area who all testified to Manno's good character and previously good name. The defense then rested.

The Commonwealth then provided their closing arguments, telling the jury that Manno admitted that he indeed had shot and killed Raffalo over something as trivial as a trowel. Driscoll said that he felt the murder was premeditated, due to the fact that

Manno had the revolver on his person, which proved that Manno's intentions were not innocent. Whitmore then provided the closing arguments for the defense. Yes, Manno had fired the shot that took Raffalo's life, but this was done in the act of self-defense and only done after Raffalo brandished his razor and threatened Manno and his wife.

Judge Hall then charged the jury with deciding whether Manno was guilty of murder in the first degree as charged by the Commonwealth, murder in the second degree, or innocent of the charges. The jury retired, and in a little, over an hour they returned with a verdict of guilty in the second degree on the charge of murder. Judge Hall thanked the jury for their services and placed the sentencing date for the April term of court. Manno was taken back to the jail to await his sentence.

On April 9th, 1910, Ralph Manno was sentenced by Judge Hall to not less than five nor more than twenty years in the Western Penitentiary. Manno served his sentence and returned to the area to live out his life. The widow of Raffalo learned of her husband's murder while still in Italy and reportedly suffered a nervous breakdown.

The Italian Princess

The grave of Susie Mart in the Holy Rosary Cemetery.

Susie Mart, the apple of her father's eye, was sixteen years old in 1919, the year Bruno Rizzo came to live with the Mart family.

Susie was described as a breathtaking Italian beauty, who turned heads everywhere she went in Johnsonburg. She was still a student in 1919 and was busy learning English, something her parents had still never accomplished, despite being in the states since 1910. As with many girls of that age, she also was developing quite an interest in the opposite sex. In this time period, girls, especially immigrant girls, married at a young age, Susie's father, Tony, was not upset when various suitors come to his house to inquire about his beautiful daughter and the possibility of arranging a marriage of such an attractive prospect. As was the rule in those days, Tony Mart expected a dowry to be paid before any plans of dating or relationship was to be discussed. The psychical charms of Susie were not unnoticed by the Mart family's boarder, Bruno Rizzo. Rizzo, of manly good looks, and with the proper Italian dialect, soon found himself enamored with Susie. After his long days of labor at the planing mill in Johnsonburg, Rizzo would appear at the Mart residence with a variety of sweet pastries for Susie and her family, in hopes of securing her hand in marriage. After Rizzo gave her mother a payment of $80 (over $1,000 in today's money), Tony allowed Rizzo to court his daughter. Susie, being of such a young age, and naturally immature, accepted Rizzo's affections and carried on as his betrothed. Rizzo had a phonograph player and a large number of records in his room. Susie would often sit with Rizzo on his bed and listen to these records. Rizzo was sure he had found his true love and worked as many hours as he could to save up for the big dowry that Mr. Mart was requesting for his daughter's hand.

Bruno Rizzo had arrived in the United States in 1914 from Italy. After taking a few menial jobs in the New York City area, he had received correspondence from a countryman who was living in Johnsonburg. Rizzo was assured he could secure a job in one of the bustling industries in Johnsonburg and had moved there with the intention of putting down roots. Rizzo secured a job at the planing mill in Johnsonburg and was described as a hard worker. Rizzo also was described as having the mind of a seven-year-old, something which would come to prominence years later. Within a year of his arrival in Johnsonburg, he had developed a friendship with one Tony Mart, a fellow immigrant from his hometown in Italy. Mart rented spare rooms in his ramshackle residence located at 426 Railroad Street, to fellow immigrants, and offered Rizzo one of these rooms. Rizzo eagerly agreed to rent the room, and he was immediately taken in by the beauty of Rizzo's teenage daughter, Susie. Rizzo, who had not learned English, was soon spending time with the young Susie, who was giving him lessons in English, which she was gleaning at school. As the two were spending more and more time together after school, a mutual infatuation developed, and Rizzo had then approached her father for his daughter's hand.

In the first few months of the "courtship," Susie enjoyed the romantic attentions of Rizzo. They were often seen walking hand in hand in the streets of Johnsonburg on weekends. Rizzo told all his fellow workmen of his determination to marry this Italian beauty, and he was described as both star struck and obsessed with Susie. Susie, meanwhile, was noticing more and more, Rizzo's infantile mental development and also noticing other Italian men who were showing her affection. Susie had accepted a small necklace as a gift from a local man of a prominent Italian family and had begun to question whether Rizzo was the man she wished to be with. She finally approached her mother and father with her concerns, and Mr. Mart decided that the choice to end the affair was her decision. Susie decided that she no longer wished to be betrothed to Rizzo. The living arrangement now became quite delicate, with Rizzo and Susie under the same roof. Rizzo would constantly follow Susie around in the house and pester her with questions and displays of affection to win her back. Mr. Mart forbid Rizzo from harassing his daughter and suggested he might as well move out if he could not contain his actions. Rizzo, who was also known to have a temper, swore that if he could not have Susie, nobody would. Rizzo then began to spend his time locked in his room, playing the records he had often shared with young Susie. Susie had meanwhile accepted the affections of another young Italian gentleman and had begun to stay out late from home, accompanying this new suitor throughout Johnsonburg. Rizzo noticed the prolonged absence of Susie and had begun to suspect she had found someone new. He was determined to find out who the new suitor was and end this relationship that he believed was rightfully his. Rizzo went to the father at this job, at the Johnsonburg Mill, and described his anguish and feelings of betrayal at the ending of his relationship with his daughter. Tony told Rizzo that if Susie no longer wished to be with him, the matter was at an end and Rizzo needed to move one. The infuriated Rizzo swore that he would kill Susie, Mrs. Mart and anyone who interfered. Mr. Mart promptly notified the authorities and the police tracked down Rizzo and notified him that he was on a warning to stay away from Susie and to no longer harass her. Rizzo promised the officer that he would stay away from Susie. Rizzo, now extremely angry at the developments of the situation, decided he would seek revenge, and end the life of young Susie.

The final catalyst for the murder came on Saturday, November 8th, 1919. Mrs. Mart had handed Rizzo back the $80 he had given the parents as a down payment on the dowry in the morning. Rizzo, angry at this final insult, vowed he would get revenge and retreated to his room. Mrs. Mart had to go to the post office and had told the young Susie to accompany her and to get her out of the residence. Susie and her mother then headed out to the post office, passing many people in the streets.

Rizzo, meanwhile, was observed through his open window, smashing his records and throwing them out of the window. He was also heard screaming that he would get revenge on Susie. Rizzo then went to the sidewalk in front of the Mart home and waited for Susie's return. Locals, who saw him, described his demeanor as nonchalant. In short order, Mrs. Mart and Susie crossed the Pennsy Railroad tracks and entered the sidewalk within a few feet of the Mart home. Rizzo promptly appeared. Mrs. Mart, sensing that trouble was imminent, headed towards Rizzo, as Rizzo sprinted towards Susie. Rizzo produced a .32 caliber revolver from his pocket and aimed it at Susie. Mrs. Mart scuffled with Rizzo and forced his hand up that held the revolver. A shot went off, hitting a fence post behind Rizzo's head. Susie watched with horror as Rizzo and Mrs. Mart wrestled over the gun. Rizzo managed to break loose from Mrs. Mart's grasp and immediately chased Susie down the sidewalk. Rizzo fired three shots at the fleeing Susie, with one shot hitting her in the abdomen as Susie turned to see how close Rizzo was to her. Susie immediately fell to the street. Rizzo quickly pocketed the smoking weapon, ran through an alley, crossed the Pennsy trestle and disappeared in the brush west of town.

Neighbors and on-lookers carried the stricken Susie into her residence, and Dr. H. H. Smith was called. Dr. Smith arrived shortly and attended to the prostate Susie, who was lying on the couch in the Mart living room, bleeding from a shot almost in the center of the abdomen. Dr. Smith realized there was nothing that could be done for the poor girl at that time and ordered her removed to the Elk County General Hospital in Ridgway. As the five o'clock express train to Ridgway was due at any time, it was decided to wait for the train, as it would be much faster and comfortable to transfer Susie than an auto. Sue arrived at the hospital shortly after five-thirty and preparations were made for immediate emergency surgery. During the surgery, it was determined that nothing could be done to save the girl, who had lost consciousness shortly after being shot. Susie Mart, aged only sixteen years, died on Monday, September 10th, 1919, less than forty-eight hours after she was shot. Death was due to complications of an infection which had set in following the stomach rupturing from Rizzo's bullet.

Susie's body was returned to Johnsonburg and was taken to the Ubel Funeral Home in preparations for the Coroner's inquest and burial. Dr. G. C. Wilson, Elk County Coroner, arrived from Saint Marys on Tuesday evening, November the 11th and appointed a coroner's jury. The jury was composed of F. B. O'Connell, foreman, H. C. Westphal, Alva Gregory, Harry Koons, A. J. Decker and W. B. Curry. Miss Magdalene Aiello acted as stenographer and Bruno Manno was the interpreter. Mrs. Mart had suffered a nervous breakdown and was unable to give her testimony to the jury. The first witness called was Mr. Tony Mart, the father of the deceased. He testified that Rizzo had boarded at his house for about a year and had made threats to kill the mother, daughter and any policeman that interfered. Some time ago, probably four or five months, Rizzo talked to him about marrying the girl. He came to the mill where Mr. Mart was employed, and Mr. Mart told him if the girl did not care for him, he might as well go away. Rizzo was extremely mad. Mr. Mart also testified that $80 that Rizzo had given to the girl's mother previously as a down payment for a dowry was given back to Rizzo on the Saturday of the shooting. Rizzo had gone up to his room at the Mart residence and had begun to smash his phonograph and records in his room.

Sam Candelero, ten years old, and a witness to the shooting was sworn next. He testified that he had known Bruno Rizzo for about a year as he was a neighbor of the Marts. He said he said he saw Rizzo smashing records in his tenement window and throwing the broken records out of the window. Candelero also saw Rizzo throw the phonograph out of his upstairs window. He said Rizzo then came out into the street and when Susie and her mother appeared, he saw the struggle and also saw the moment Rizzo fired the weapon at the fleeing Susie.

Sam Vallone, fifteen years old, was then sworn in. Vallone testified that he saw the gun in Rizzo's hand and that he witnessed the struggle with Mrs. Mart and the subsequent shooting by Rizzo. He also testified that he last saw Rizzo fleeing down the tracks headed towards Ridgway.

Louis Onsor, eleven years old, testified that he was on the train track by the fence when he saw Bruno Rizzo chasing the Mart girl and heard a gunshot. Onsor said he saw the Mart girl collapse and saw Rizzo immediately head down the train tracks where he disappeared into the brush. Onsor said it all happened so quickly, that nobody thought of following Rizzo.

Mrs. Rose Candelero was sworn next. She said she lives fifteen feet from the Mart house, and saw Rizzo pull out the revolver and shoot. She testified that she was on one side of Rizzo, while Mrs. Mart was on the other side of Rizzo. She said she heard Rizzo exclaim in Italian that if he did not marry Susie Mart, no one would.

Bruno Manno was sworn next. He said he was at the lower mill gate and heard four shots, and then screams. He then saw Susie Mart lying on the sidewalk. He asked Susie who had shot her and she answered "Bruno!" Susie then lost consciousness and never spoke again. The crowd that had gathered said it was Bruno Rizzo. Manno also testified that he did not see Bruno Rizzo at the scene of the shooting.

The jury then viewed the body of Susie Mart and then rendered the verdict that: "Susie Mart then and there lying dead, came to her death from a gunshot wound from a revolver in the hands of Bruno Rizzo."

The funeral services for Susie Mart were held on Wednesday morning from the Holy Rosary Catholic Church in Johnsonburg, with a large group of mourner's present. Susie, who was born in Italy, was survived by her parents, Tony and Rosa Mart, as well as three sisters, Mary, Theresia and Carmella, and one brother Andrew. Pallbearers were Frank Galeazzo, Frank Torchia, Frank Messenger, Frank Burello, Dominick Garlate, and Paul Mouerdo. A solemn procession took place, with burial in the Catholic Cemetery at Wardvale.

Meanwhile, the manhunt for Bruno Rizzo had been taking place. The authorities had speculated that Rizzo had made careful preparations for his escape prior to the shooting of Susie. He was last seen running down the railroad tracks heading towards Ridgway and was noticed to disappear in the brush which was located alongside the railroad tracks. When the police searched his room at the Mart house, all they found was a large trunk in his room. The trunk only contained a straw hat and a bunch of letters. These letters would later provide a clue to the eventual whereabouts of Rizzo. Police also found a shotgun, which Rizzo, being an un-naturalized citizen, constituted an extra felony charge. The rest of his possessions he had broken and scattered outside his window. The authorities had provided a good description of Rizzo and forwarded this description to all locales throughout Elk County. It was surmised that Rizzo had headed towards Ridgway either following the railroad tracks or had followed Montmorenci Road into Ridgway. With the return address of the letter's found in Rizzo's room, the police speculated that Rizzo would be heading in the direction of

Pittsburgh. The first break in the case came when a man by the name of Hoffman, who lived in Portland Mills, telephoned the police to tell his story. He phoned Deputy Sheriff May in Ridgway on Saturday evening and said he was driving his auto home from Ridgway when he met a man answering Rizzo's description, south of Ridgway, and offered him a ride. The stranger rode with Hoffman as far as Carman, where he said he was going to Brockwayville. Rizzo made it to Brockwayville and purchased a ticket to Pittsburgh on the night flyer. Sheriff May alerted the State Police that Rizzo was heading in the direction of Pittsburgh on the train and to arrest him as soon as he was sighted. Rizzo was considered to be armed and dangerous. The State Police set up surveillance on the train station at Woodlawn, which was thirty to forty miles this side of Pittsburgh, to await the arrival of the train. Rizzo was easily discovered amongst the passengers on the train and was taken into custody without resistance. Rizzo was taken to the Beaver County Jail in Beaver Falls. *The Butler Citizen* described Rizzo as "having the peculiar "Charlie Chaplin" shuffle, which Bruno Rizzo cannot overcome in his walking, caused his apprehension Monday by State Troopers for the alleged murder of sixteen-year-old Susie Mart at Johnsonburg." The State Police telephoned Deputy May in Ridgway and informed him that Rizzo was captured and was being held in the Beaver County Jail. Deputy May left Ridgway on Tuesday night headed towards Beaver Falls and returned Wednesday with Rizzo in his custody. Rizzo was hastily arraigned in Ridgway and lodged in the Elk County Jail without bail, pending trial for the murder of young Susie Mart.

The trial of Bruno Rizzo took place on Monday, April 4th, 1921, in the Elk County Courthouse in Ridgway. Judge R. B. McCormick was the presiding judge. District Attorney McFarlin represented the Commonwealth. Attorneys Dennis Driscoll of Saint Marys and Byron F. Ely of Ridgway were appointed to defend Rizzo. The prosecution had declared that this would be a first-degree murder case with the death penalty sought. The jury chosen included: Joseph Brem from Fox township, G. C. Hoffman from Benzinger township, S.S. Rank from Johnsonburg, Charles Larkin, from Caledonia, Edward Van Ordsdall from Ridgway township, I. C. Weidenboerner from Saint Marys, William Brut from Weedville, Otto Zelt from Saint Marys, Andrew Gier from Ridgway, C. W. DeHaas from Johnsonburg, William Miller from Saint Marys and J. C. Maloney from Weedville. The prosecution present that this was a premeditated murder and that Rizzo carefully planned the murder and his subsequent escape well ahead of the actual shooting.

The defense countered that this was a case of "hot blood." The plan to shoot Susie only formed in the heat of passion as the result of Susie's rejection of Rizzo's affection. As there was no premeditation, he was guilty of murder in the second degree at most. The charge of first-degree murder was not warranted. The trial lasted three full days with the case going to the jury shortly before five o'clock on Wednesday afternoon, April the 6th. During the three-day trial, the prosecution called all of the witnesses that were presented at the coroner's jury, as well as Deputy Sheriff May who testified that Rizzo had made a confession on the train ride, they took back to Ridgway from Beaver Falls. Rizzo did not testify in his defense at the trial and was also noticed to have remained unnaturally quiet throughout the proceedings, never speaking to his defense attorneys, except for brief answers to their whispered questions. The defense, meanwhile, presented a strenuous argument that while Rizzo did indeed commit the shooting, he did so in the throes of extreme passion, and that the jury should take this into consideration, as Rizzo was not guilty of first-degree murder, and they should set aside this verdict in favor of second-degree murder and life imprisonment. The jury retired for only 18 minutes and returned with a verdict of guilty of murder in the first degree. The jury also recommended that Rizzo should suffer the punishment of death for his crime. Judge McCormick concurred with the jury's findings and passed on the penalty of death. Both Driscoll and Ely promised an appeal of this verdict and sentence. Rizzo appeared unfazed by the verdict and was escorted back to his jail cell.

Immediately after the trial, Driscoll and Ely filed a motion with the Board of Pardons, that Rizzo should not be executed as he was not only not guilty of first-degree murder but possessed the mentality of a child and was therefore not responsible for his actions. The appeal filed by Driscoll and Ely stated that "the judgment was against the weight of the evidence which did not warrant or justify a verdict of guilty of murder in the first degree. The court erred in refusing the defendants' request for a general exception to the charge to the jury. The reasonable doubt as to the deliberate, willful and premeditated murder was not sufficiently explained to the jury by the judge in the general chare, and the "jury should have been more fully instructed as the weight they should have given to defendants' testimony bearing upon his mental incapacity to premeditate the killing, so as to reduce the homicide from murder in the first degree to that of the second degree."

The actions of Rizzo and his conduct before the shooting were the basis of the motion. Further evidence of his behavior after his commitment to jail and during the time he was on trial for his life was also part of the appeal. This behavior had led his attorneys and friends to believe he is an imbecile, and as such, was unable to manage himself or his affairs with ordinary prudence. Dr. H. W. Mitchell, of the Warren State Hospital for the Insane, and Dr. J. M. Murdoch, of the State Institution for the feeble-minded at Polk, who were both considered expert alienists and specialists in mental diseases, made personal examinations of the condemned after the verdict was rendered. Both of the Doctors found that Rizzo was congenitally mentally defective, though he is physically a well-developed young man. They found he was densely ignorant, displayed most primitive ideas of moral, ethical concepts and in response to the recognized psychological tests in common use for the determining the capacity of an individual, he did not show mental development beyond that commonly found in a child eight or ten years old. Rizzo's control of his affairs or regulating his reactions to others was also to be expected that he would show no more than childlike judgments or self-control. As the board of pardons was able to intervene in the higher board of justice and humanity, was the reason the defense attorneys appealed to the board of pardons, as well as an appeal to the State Supreme Court. A petition was also presented to the Board of Pardons which was signed by many leading citizens of Johnsonburg. The hearing was held on May 19th, 1921 in Harrisburg. Driscoll and Ely presented their evidence that Rizzo was mentally challenged and also provided the expert testimony of the alienists. After hearing the evidence presented, the board took the pardon into consideration and retired to render a verdict on the commutation in the near future. On Thursday, July 10, 1920, the Pardon Board, after reviewing the evidence presented as to the incompetency of Rizzo, agreed to the petition of Driscoll and Ely and commuted the sentence from death to life imprisonment for Rizzo. Rizzo, still residing in the Elk County Jail while his appeal was active, was reportedly pleased with this ruling.

Bruno Rizzo was transported to the Western Penitentiary to serve his life sentence. Rizzo was again in the news in 1940 when he applied for a pardon, after having served twenty-one years.

Rizzo was described as having been employed in the shoe cobbler's shop at the Penitentiary, and his attorney John Ray, told the board "He has served half a normal lifetime in prison. He may be ready now to be given an opportunity to live outside prison walls." A friend, Leonard Pematta, of Aliquippa, also offered to employ Rizzo in his shoemaking shop should he be released. Rizzo's request was denied, and he continued to toil in the cobbler's shop at the prison. This was his second appeal, the first having been applied for in 1936.

Rizzo once again appealed for commutation of his sentence in 1944. This time he was successful in his request, and Governor Martin commuted the sentence on December 16th of 1944. Rizzo left the prison and relocated to Aliquippa with his friend. His whereabouts after his release from parole in the 1950s is not known.

The Infamous Skeleton

Adam Ruth, alias Frank Barnes

In the history of Elk County, finding bodies and skeletons of unknown people was once a regular occurrence. When I was researching the murders in the coroner's archives, I often found details of bodies who had been recovered, but whom a name was never given. Some of these people had died of drowning, some had been hit by trains and automobiles, and some had simply been found in the underbrush of the County. When a body was found hidden, the authorities knew it was a suspicious case and warranted further investigation. More often than not, these supposed murders were discovered by accident, and although the cause of death such as a gunshot could be readily detected, the name of the deceased was never uncovered, and the case became unsolved for all of eternity. The bodies that were easily found were also meant to be found. The following is one such case in which all was not as it appeared. The skeleton was not hidden and bore no signs of obvious deliberate trauma. The authorities came up with several scenarios on how the man met his death, but they would find out later that they were dead wrong in their suppositions, or were they?

On Sunday, August the 23rd, 1908, Charles and William Bartholomew from Saint Marys headed out towards the Elk County Home on Washington Street to pick blackberries. The young boys told their mother that they would not be late and would return as soon as they filled their buckets. Mrs. Bartholomew promised to bake a pie as soon as they returned with the berries. The boys went to an area locally known as Maple Glen, which was situated on the right side of the P. S. & N. Railroad tracks, approximately three-quarters of a mile from the County Home. As the boys filled their buckets with berries, Charles leaned down to pick some low hanging fruit and noticed a pair of shoes lying in the underbrush. He thought this was quite peculiar and called his brother over to investigate. Lying in the leaves, partially uncovered, was a bleached white skull attached to a skeleton dressed in torn and ratty clothing and shoes. The boys did not waste any time surveying the gruesome find and hightailed it back to their house, where they told their mother of what they had discovered. Mrs. Bartholomew immediately informed the authorities. Dr. C. G. Wilson and the local police hastened to Maple Glen, where they were joined by

Elk County Home Superintendent Dr. J. W. De Haas, on whose property the skeleton was found.

What the group was looking at appeared to be the bones of a rather large man. The skeleton was clad in a tattered black shirt, brown corduroy pants and a pair of heavy laced shoes. The bones were bleached almost pure white, leading the investigators to surmise that the deceased had lain at this location for a lengthy time, estimated to have been over two years. A search of the skeleton's pockets and the immediate area turned up no clue as to his identification. The authorities also could find no sign of trauma. Dr. Wilson made arrangements for the remains to be taken to the Meisel Funeral Parlor for a more thorough examination.

The authorities began to attempt to identify the body. One missing local man, Bert Brendel, of Kersey, was mentioned as a possible match. Brendel had left his residence in Brandy Camp some two years prior and had not been heard from since. Relatives of the missing man were contacted, and arrangements were made for them to come to the funeral home to view the clothing that was found on the skeleton, in the hopes that they would be able to identify the corpse as their beloved family member. The Brendel family emphatically said that the clothes found with the skeleton were not those that were worn by their loved one when he disappeared. The authorities sent out a description of the clothes to local law enforcement agencies and quietly arranged for the burial of the bones at the Elk County Home Cemetery. The skull of the dead man was given to a local dentist to use as an educational tool. As the finding of an unknown body was a regular occurrence and that although the skull appeared to have a broken nose, the authorities ruled the death as an accident. Dr. Wilson listed one of his theories of death, being that the man had taken a drink from the nearby sulfur ridden stream and had become sick. The man had lay down in the leaves and perished during the night. The discovery of the remains was hampered by the heavy coating of leaves that permeated the area where the bones were found. The case of the unidentified skeleton was then closed, only to be reopened in the case that some other missing person was reported with the same type of clothes as the deceased. The authorities would not have to wait long before the identity of the skeleton would be disclosed, in an almost unbelievable and important investigation taking place in another county.

Frank Barnes, of no permanent adobe, was a perfect example of a criminal. He had served some seven to eight terms in the Western Penitentiary for crimes he had committed ranging from armed robbery to arson to attempted manslaughter. No matter what type of treatment or sentence he received for his crimes, Barnes returned to the only life he knew, one of crime. In July of 1908, Barnes was arrested for a robbery at Pithole, in Venango County. He was taken to the Venango County Jail to await trial, and this is when he began his fabulous confessions. Barnes, well known for previous crimes in the area, was also considered somewhat of a liar and braggart, whose words should be taken with a grain of salt. While in the jail, Barnes was questioned by the county detective as to the whereabouts of his accomplice in the recent robbery. Barnes, angry that he was the only one arrested, and also angry that only a small amount of cash was taken during the robbery, decided to get even with his partner in crime. Barnes named his accomplice as one Daniel Wilder, another well know criminal, and Barnes said he could be found in Bradford, PA. Barnes named the location in Bradford of their "hideout" and also claimed that Wilder kept a "fence" in Bradford where an untold amount of plunder was kept. The authorities at once went to Bradford and arrested Wilder at the exact location that Barnes had specified. The whereabouts of the "fence" was not discovered at this time and whether it was ever found was never disclosed. Wilder now joined Barnes in the county lockup, although the two were separated, lest the two attempted to harm each other. Barnes then began a series of astonishing confessions which implicated his former partner in crime in some of the most infamous and unsolved homicides to have occurred in these parts of Pennsylvania.

Barnes, who went by many aliases, implicated his partner Wilder out of resentment that he had been set up several times for crimes by Wilder and had served lengthy prison sentences in each case due to the treachery of Wilder. The present arrest was the straw that broke his back, and he was determined to bring Wilder down. As Barnes continued his confessions of wild armed robberies and burglaries carried out by Wilder, the authorities began to discount some of the stories as being untrue, after doing some investigations. Barnes swore everything he was telling them he had heard from Wilder. It should be noted, that during the time periods for every crime he implicated Wilder having committed, Barnes was incarcerated in the Western Penitentiary, and thereby not a part of the act. Barnes then decided to change the scope of his information from robberies to murder. Barnes stated that Wilder had often posed as a salesman of ointments and perfumes and had gained access to unsuspecting victims in their homes when he went door to door. While in these homes, he surveyed the situations and surroundings and plotted the easiest escape route for when he came back to burglarize them. Barnes said that Wilder had told him of two such instances in Clarion County that ended up in murder. Barnes said that Wilder confessed to him that he had slain Mrs. Eberhart and her daughter-in-law Mrs. Gilfian in the village of Fryburg, during the commission of one of these burglaries in 1886. Barnes also said that Wilder was responsible for the murder of the wealthy hermit, Kiser, at Elk Springs, in

1899, a crime for which the "West Shore Gang" was accused of at the turn of the century. The Venango Authorities checked with the Clarion County Authorities and did indeed find that these murders had taken place and were unsolved. As Barnes could provide no substantial clues and Wilder was vehemently denying anything to do with these murders, the authorities did not consider Barnes credible. When questioning Barnes as to the inconsistencies of the stories that Wilder supposedly confessed to him, Barnes made the startling statement that he could and would prove that Wilder was involved in the 1899 unsolved murder of New Castle City Treasurer, John Blevin. This aroused great excitement with the authorities, as this was the greatest unsolved murder in Laurence County and indeed most of the state. Barnes said he could prove what he was saying was the truth and he began to offer crucial details.

According to Barnes, he was in New Castle around the time of the murder of City Treasurer Blevins, and that he met Wilder and two accomplices who told him their plans of robbing the treasurer's office. Barnes said he was planning to take part in the deed but had to go to Franklin to take care of some business and was arrested on the way to Franklin on an outstanding warrant. Barnes said that when he was in the Franklin Jail, he learned of the robbery and death of Blevins. He said after serving four years in the State Penitentiary, he was released around 1905 and met up with Wilder in their hometown of Olean, New York, where he once again became acquainted with Wilder. It was then that Wilder told him that he was the mastermind of the New Castle Murder. Barnes went on to say that in short order, he was again arrested for the abduction and rape of a young girl and once again found himself in the State Penitentiary, only being released several months before his present arrest. Barnes again sought out Wilder, and Wilder divulged more details of the New Castle crime. According to

Barnes, Wilder told him that he was accompanied in the crime by two individuals, William Farrell, and Eugene Parker. After the robbery and subsequent murder of Treasurer Blevins, the group had broken up, with Wilder carrying a substantial amount of money and promises to divide the loot at a later date. Wilder traveled to Bradford, while the other two individuals traveled towards Clearfield. Wilder supposedly hid the bulk of the proceeds in his secret stash in Bradford, and when the men met up some time after the murder, he gave them each what amounted to $1,000. Parker was not accepting of this amount and said he saw much more money in the looted safe during the robbery. Wilder told him to shut his mouth, or he would be sorry. Wilder ended up getting arrested for a different robbery and was placed in the State Penitentiary for several years, only being released in 1906. While he was in prison, he had heard through friends that Parker was bad mouthing him about the New Castle robbery and that Wilder had shorted him from the proceeds. Wilder also heard that Parker had taken to drink, and often bragged to complete strangers of his complicity in the New Castle murder. Wilder, upon being released, hunted down Parker in Clearfield, and at first, he befriended him. Wilder supposedly lured Parker to Saint Marys and suggested they take a walk along the railroad tracks to scope out a new burglary he was planning. When the pair reached a point on the tracks, known locally as Maple Glen, Wilder suggested that the duo sit on a stump to discuss their latest venture and share in some whiskey Wilder had brought along. Wilder then had hit Parker with a club and finished the job by strangling the man to death. Wilder then hid the body under some leaves and hopped the train headed towards Olean. Wilder specifically told Barnes that the dead man Parker was clad in brown corduroy pants and a black shirt. Wilder also asked Barnes to go to Saint Marys upon his release from prison, in June of 1908 and to bury the body of Parker with quick lime so it could never be found. Barnes stated that he planned on doing this, but his latest arrest had prevented it.

The Venango County authorities were baffled by all of these accusations and implications offered by Barnes. When the stories of the murders in Clarion County checked out, they decided that there may be something to Barnes' stories. When they queried the New Castle Police, they at first received promising reviews, but these quickly turned to disdain, as the authorities there did not believe that these common criminals were in any way responsible for what they saw as an inside job. In October of 1908, the Venango Authorities then contacted the Elk County Authorities and queried if a skeleton had ever been discovered in Saint Marys, at a location called Maple Glen? The Elk County Authorities answered in the affirmative and stated that the skeleton had only been found in August and had been buried at the local poor house property. The description of the clothes matched that provided by Barnes, down to and including the brown corduroy pants and a black shirt. The bones were also of a large man, just as Barnes had described Parker. The locale also matched the spot where Barnes said the murder took place. The Venango Authorities traveled with Barnes to Saint Marys and followed his directions to Maple Glen, recounting to them from what Wilder had allegedly told him. A name was now placed on the unknown skeleton, one Eugene Parker, aged about fifty and from parts unknown. The party traveled back to Franklin by train and felt assured that they had the missing link to the Blevin murder.

Meanwhile, in the Venango County Jail, Dan Wilder was relentlessly interrogated on all of the mounting accusations proposed by Barnes. Wilder emphatically denied any knowledge of any of the slayings and said he had never been to New Castle in his life. His persistent denials were not unexpected from such a career criminal, but the authorities decided they needed more evidence to arrest him on the Blevin murder charge. This was when Barnes made a fatal mistake in his alleged testimony. Around the time of the Blevin murder, newspaper articles had said that a substantial amount of bonds, payable to a local farmer, had been among the items stolen during the burglary. A future press release had said these same bonds had been anonymously delivered to the bankrupt farmer, who was facing foreclosure due to the loss of these bonds. The article went on to say that whoever murdered Blevin must still have had a heart and upon hearing of the misfortune, had decided to return the bonds and make the farmer whole again. Barnes reencountered this story and said that Wilder had told him that he was the one who returned the bonds via an anonymous post. This is where Barnes story fell apart. Unknown to the public, the story of the missing bonds and their anonymous return was a total fabrication. No bonds in a farmer's name were ever stolen, and this story was planted in the media at the time to develop an interest in what was fast becoming a cold case. This slip by Barnes made the authorities believe that all that Barnes had told them, he had learned from reading the newspapers of the time. It was believed that all of his sensational revelations were made up in an attempt to get revenge on one Dan Wilder, a man he believed had wronged him one too many times. Barnes had made all of these allegations up in order to get a lenient sentence for the burglary he was now in prison for. Barnes ended up getting just what he wanted. When it came time for sentencing in the Venango burglary charge, Barnes was spared time at the State Penitentiary and sentenced to serve his time in the local Franklin Jail. Wilder, on the other hand, received a State Prison term of six years for his masterminding and participation in the same robbery.

No-one was ever prosecuted for the murder of John Blevins in New Castle. Wilder served his prison term and returned to the Bradford area as an old man, but still, one involved in crime. Barnes too served many more prison terms and was last heard of resorting to the crime of extortion, for which he was quickly caught and once again sentenced to prison. Barnes had extorted money in 1911 from the parents of the young Adams and Steffan boys, who went missing in 1910. Barnes said he had information that would locate the boys, but this was just another one of his fairy tales. Was the skeleton found in Saint Marys that of one Eugene Parker? And if so, who killed him and why? I personally believe that Barnes had read the account of the finding of the skeleton in the newspaper while he was incarcerated in the Venango County Jail. The story of the discovery was widely covered in the news at the time and gave an accurate description of what the clothes the skeleton was clad in, including the brown corduroy pants. If Barnes did not read this in the paper, then he most certainly was involved in the death of this man.

Clark's Mills

The train station at Straight, around the time of the shooting

In 1910 the Town of Straight was in decline. The lumber industry was winding down operations in the area, as most of the trees had been harvested. On the lower end of Straight was a large mill which had been built by the Clark Brothers from New York. The Mill included a large saw operation, a log stripping component and a pond. This area was popularly known as Clark's Mills. Today this area is submerged under the East Branch Dam. Most of the workers had already departed the Mill in search of other employment, with just a few employees retained to close down the operations. Although there were taverns in Straight, the men who lived there often traveled to nearby Glen Hazel to consume alcohol and for a change of scenery. The men would often return in the early morning hours, full of alcohol, and loud and raucous in their behavior.

On Friday night, April 1st, 1910, one of these workers was making his way back to Straight and his residence located in the lumber camp by Clarks Mills. The lumber camp consisted of several buildings which housed the workers in a communal type setting. William, "Bill," Chamberlin, had spent the night drinking whiskey in Glen Hazel and had made his way back to Clark's Mills sometime close to midnight. The night of April the 1st was particularly dark, as no moon was visible, and the area was blanketed by snow and cloud cover. A local resident, Sylvester Burke, had retired for the night and was in a deep sleep when he heard a loud knocking at his door. Burke, an elderly, gentleman, went to his door and inquired of whom was creating such a commotion at such a late hour. The intruder yelled at Burke to open up the door and let him in. The intruder refused to identify himself and instead ordered Burke to open up the door. Burke told the intruder to leave at once, or he would get his gun. Chamberlin refused to leave and instead began to ram his large body against the door, with the intention of breaking the door down. Burke hastened to secure his rifle, and just as he turned around, Chamberlin burst through the door. Burke fired a single bullet at Chamberlin's chest, and Chamberlin died before his body hit the floor.

Sylvester Burke was employed by the Clark Brothers for over fifteen years and was the supervisor charged with closing down the mill operations and securing the brothers' property for eventual liquidation. Sylvester was in his late sixties and although of advanced age, was still quite a physically active gentleman. Sylvester was also known as a teetotaler, who had a gentle disposition, as well as having a sense of right and wrong.

William Chamberlin was fifty-two in 1910. He had moved to Elk County, specifically Ridgway, back in the 1890s in search of employment in the lumber camps that were plentiful throughout the County. Chamberlin came from a well to do family in Buffalo, New York. He had one brother who still lived in Buffalo. His brother was a medical doctor, and they had regular contact. Chamberlin was described as a hard worker as well as a hard drinker. He was known to often participate in alcohol-fueled fights on the weekends when he was not working as a lumberman.

Sylvester, moments before in a deep sleep, now peered down at the prone body of a stranger stretched out in his doorway. Burke checked the man's vitals and found he was deceased. He knew that what had happened could be considered a crime and immediately knew he had to inform the authorities of the happenings. Burke quickly dressed and drug the body into his living quarters, so he could secure the door. He then headed towards Glen Hazel in the early morning light. In Glen Hazel, he visited some of his friends and told them of what had happened and how he wanted to turn himself into the authorities. Glen Hazel authorities phoned the Elk County Coroner, as Burke started out towards Johnsonburg, where he planned to give himself up at the Jail. Burke turned himself into the Johnsonburg Constable and was in turn placed in the local jail until the findings of an investigation. Elk County Coroner Sharpe went to Clark's Mills and held an inquest into the death at Burke's residence, with the body of Chamberlin present. The Coroner found that Chamberlin had died of a gunshot wound to the heart. The Coroner's jury found that Chamberlin came to his death by a gunshot wound caused by Sylvester Burke. Chamberlin's body was removed to the Ubel Funeral Home in Johnsonburg to be prepared for burial. The Elk County Commissioners attempted to contact Chamberlin's physician brother in Buffalo without success. Burke was meanwhile taken into custody at the Johnsonburg Jail by Elk County Sheriff's Deputy May, who transported him to the Elk County Jail.

A full coroner's inquest was held at the Elk County Jail on Thursday, April the 7th, in Ridgway. The only witness heard, besides the coroner, was Sylvester Burke, who was held at the Jail. Burke gave his story of how Chamberlin had repeatedly refused to leave his residence despite Burke telling him to leave or face the consequences. Burke also told of how he did not personally know Chamberlin and had never been in an altercation with him previously. Burke also told the jury of how he only fired his weapon when Chamberlin had broken down his door and entered in a rage. After hearing the evidence, the jury found that William Chamberlin had come to his death at the hands of Sylvester Burke in the process of breaking and entering his residence. The jury further found that the shooting was justified and that no charges were to be filed against Burke as it was a case of self-defense. Burke was then released from jail and headed back to Clark Mill's and his employment. The Elk County Commissioners had meanwhile finally been able to contact Chamberlin's brother in Buffalo, but he was not interested in claiming his brother's body, and Chamberlin was buried in an unmarked grave at the Rolfe Cemetery.

Chamberlin's Death Certificate

ACKNOWLEDGMENTS

I would like to thank all of you, my cherished readers, who provided so much positive feedback on Volume I. You have given me the inspiration to continue this project. Thanks also to the Johnsonburg Public Library and the Elk County Historical Society for the use of their materials. Thanks also to my love Lynn for all you do.

OTHER FINE BOOKS AVAILABLE FROM BAUMGRATZ PUBLISHING, LLC

elkcountymurder.com

- *Tiger at the Bar, The Life Story of Charles Margiotti* by Chester Harris
- *Elk County, A Journey through time* by John Imhof
- *Gettysburg Day 2, A study in Maps* by John Imhof
- *History of Capital Crimes, Confessions and Death Penalties in Clearfield County 1816 – 1914*
- *Elk County Murders & Mysterious Deaths, Volume I*

COMING SOON:

A Story of the Sinnamahone (Reprint) 1936

Order Form

Please send Check or Money Order to:

Baumgratz Publishing, LLC
P.O. Box 100
Ridgway, PA 15853

Title	Cost Each	Total
Elk County Murders Volume I	$24.95	_____
Elk County Murders Volume II	$24.95	_____
Tiger at the Bar	$42.95	_____
Elk County Journey Through Time	$24.95	_____
History of Capital Crimes, Clearfield	$8.95	_____
Gettysburg Day 2, A Study in Maps	$49.95	_____
Shipping and Handling:		$3.99
Total Enclosed:	$_____	

Please enclose your Name, Address, and email address.

Thank You for Your Order!